THE
GREATER
PURPOSE

Awaken to Your Reason for Being

Robyn G. Locke

GIVEN BY THE ELDERS

The Greater Purpose: Awaken to Your Reason for Being
Published by Golden Page Publishing
Atlanta, GA

ISBN: 978-0-9992458-1-1 (Amazon)
ISBN: 979-8-9877542-2-1 (Ingram)

Library of Congress Control Number: 2022947444
BODY, MIND & SPIRIT / Inspiration & Personal Growth

QUANTITY PURCHASES: Schools, companies, professional groups, clubs, and other organizations may qualify for special terms when ordering quantities of this title. Email info@AdvancedEnergetics.org for more details.

THE GREATER PURPOSE

Table of Contents

Foreword
Moving Forward into All that Is

As we set about this day to bring all into unity and oneness, we ask you to embrace these words and teachings in a way of allowing a remembering to bubble up and occur within your being. For you see, this has been an objective for perhaps more than simply this lifetime. And we want you to experience and know that which you sought to know once upon a time.

And so, as you delve into these writings, into these teachings, into these understandings, know that more exists within your being and world. And perhaps more than you may recognize today.

And so, when you enter into these teachings and quite simply these past things that you once knew, know that all awaits your discovery. And in the bubbling up which will certainly occur, set the intention that it may do so. Set the intention that each word reverberates with clarity, promise, and purpose.

For you see, all awaits discovery and your rediscovery.

All awaits that which you purposefully, intentfully, will-fully, and lovingly embrace. And that is what we seek to impart here. We seek for you to know that you are more than you may believe to be today. And that all is possible within the realm of all that you attract into your life by the thoughts you keep. By the way you look upon life in the perspective that you hold. And by the whimsical wonder-ings and meanderings that you set up to consider rather than those that the mind may interject into your life path.

And so recognize this. Recognize that you are so much more than the physical aspect that you know to be you. And so this day, we await your engagement — we await your wondering — we await all that is to spring forth now in this time as you move to embrace a greater understand-ing than perhaps you knew before. And we await seeing what you will see and know to be true as you complete the reason for your being in this time-space continuum. We welcome that awareness. We welcome that new awareness as we welcome *all that is*.

— the Elders

In Appreciation

I cannot imagine life without the Love, support, and guidance of the Elders. I am in constant awe of their words, the Loving energy they emit, and the new insights they allow me to glean. In sharing from their unique vantage, my perspectives in life have changed accordingly. They are my most valued and treasured resource, lifeline, gift. They are the reason I can't wait for each day to unfold as I discover something wonderful and previously unknown. It is for this unique purpose that I strive for more to be. It is the allness in all that I do as I seek to be and discover more.

I am grateful for my Mother. In life, she was a spiritual trailblazer. She continually sought to discover more. She never accepted a status quo sort of existence, nor did she limit how she sought to understand more. Growing up, she was my spiritual role model and mentor. Mom physically passed, making her transition in 2020. I appreciate her unabashed desire to look beyond the more rigid belief system which existed during my early youth as she sought to discover more.

Thank you to Sue, Peggy, and Diane for your ongoing support and friendship. A big thank you to Lorie, Victoria, Lorna, Polly, and John for making this book and its audio companion possible.

Might you be in that space of Loving embrace, acceptance, and allowing as you consider now a bit more regarding your own unique history. Use this book as a springboard for your upcoming and customized adventure. Allow purposeful realizations to bubble up to the surface as you seek to discover and enact more.

THE GREATER PURPOSE
Book One: The Purpose Trilogy

The Little Book to
FIND YOUR PURPOSE

When All Aligns for You

Robyn G. Locke
GIVEN BY THE ELDERS

THE LITTLE BOOK TO FIND YOUR PURPOSE

Table of Contents

Preface

We seek to provide fundamental knowledge as you begin to consciously co-create your present moment and all the steps that move beyond it.

Surrender to create the possibilities you seek as you move into the expansiveness of what might be as you live from the vantage of possibility and purpose.

Here you will find simple yet profound building blocks to shift the way you perceive and receive insights so you might move mountains, manifest rapidly and co-exist in the synergy of Now.

How to Receive to Perceive

D o you see that all is possible when you begin from the heart space? Begin in that way each time you read here. Ask for clarity and understanding. Set the intention that more is to be. Set the intention to read with your heart as opposed to your head. Seek and ye shall find. Move in an unbridled way. Each time you stop or pause reading, begin again by focusing on your heart and asking for more to be. Ask for more to be understood, and that you move always in the clarity of Love.

Given by the Elders

Chapter 1

The Synergy of Now

Each day begins anew. This allows for a world filled with new opportunities and their possibilities to be explored. Synergistic qualities exist in all things. Imagine planting a seed into the ground. If you want to grow an apple tree, you would not plant an orange seed in your orchard. What you plant, spend time on, and nurture is what will grow. If an apple seed is planted, it will not bear the fruit of an orange tree. Remember, too, as you move forward each day, you choose how to proceed and what you want to bring into your life. Your choices are as seeds that mature and grow to become fruit-bearing trees, producing like-kind fruit that will be succulent or sour based upon the variety planted. How you feed them will determine their health, vigor, and production.

As you consider your purpose now, do certain things

bring you joy and a feeling of expansiveness? Then you will want to do more of the things that align with your positive, uplifted feelings.

As you make choices, you are exercising one of humanity's greatest gifts, which is free will. With this gift, you can choose to follow this or that path, spend time in one way or another, enjoy or not enjoy something. If better feelings come from doing a kindness to another person, rather than experiencing bad feelings when being unkind to another, you probably will choose to do those things that make you feel better. Focus your thoughts on what provides happier feelings.

Understand, too, that free will is a most significant occurrence. Its importance is not fully appreciated, especially when you want to do what's best. Each decision is significant because it sets you on a trajectory which incrementally does change the direction of your life. Even the smallest choice contributes to your life's course. Small decisions lead to bigger ones, and the momentum they create is sometimes hard to stop — although easier to redirect. If you are making choices that resonate with your inner being, you are moving more in the direction sketched out before your Soul came into this body to experience this life.

Choices do impact everything within your life as you reap the rewards or consequences from each decision made. Your life, your outer reality, is a reflection of your inner being. The choices you decide to focus upon today play a big role in how you feel. So what you think, what you bring into your awareness — each plays a role in your world. And it all begins with a simple choice.

It is because of the decisions made that Universe returns back to you what you have called forth. You are a co-creator in this world of form. Do you realize that where you reside today, both physically and mentally, is the result of all decisions that have led you here?

How you align yourself and where you place your focus does, in turn, manifest things similar to the vibration you have set into motion. This will, in effect, return (to you) more of what you seemingly desire. But does your focus reside on wanted or unwanted things? For example, you thought about something you did not want, and now it is here. So simple to bring it into your life, especially when you do not hold any opposition to the thoughts you are thinking. Thus, you can unknowingly manifest.

So you see, although you want one aspect to be in your life, you have drawn forth something that might quite literally be its opposite. It is what you feel, and those feelings do evoke themselves from words spoken. Words spoken, felt, internalized, and forgotten. These are the workings of emotions and their trapped aspects that lie dormant for a time until they manifest in your world. All you have created must be felt and recognized before a release can occur.

Emotions are for humanity, a means to know what path they are on and if they have made decisions in keeping with their desired course of direction. How do your thoughts and their related actions make you feel? You may have heard it said — *If it doesn't feel good, choose a different thought.* Choose to think and do those things that make you feel good and generally more at peace with life.

From this vantage, know you are meant to experience life with all of its trappings, not just certain things. This is the actual reason you have incarnated into this physical form. You have come here to experience life and to fully feel all of your creations. Not to think you know how something feels as if you were reading a textbook, but to actually feel the emotions created by embracing each experience.

Do you believe much of the world revolves around you, and even in another's story, you are somehow in the midst of what is being shared? Do you try to find the similarity or correlation? Are they telling you this story to make some point about you?

You use your life experience filters to define a story a friend shares and any special meaning behind their story. By the time their storytelling is finished, you have created some drama on various points, but you do not stop to clarify these nuances. You allow for the continuation of the story, and soon the conversation has changed focus. As in most social settings, you move onto another topic.

Shortly you lose recall of the specific points within the story that may have ruffled your feathers. Yet the body remembers you had some angst on various points. So not able to fully feel the effects of the words that were spoken, these soundbites and the emotions they stirred in you when left unexpressed became stored, tucked down, and layered upon.

In time, this trapped energy will gather more of its kind, resurfacing as an ache, pain, or some other discomfort. *Gee, I wasn't doing anything to have caused this pain ... why is this happening to me? What did I do to cause this?* These things were caused by former, unexpressed thoughts, emotions, and the feelings they equated to when internalized. Acknowledge and feel each thing to enable a quick release to occur.

Once felt, each energetic creation can melt away and dissipate. Otherwise, this energy, known as emotions, may remain trapped. They do energetically shift all within their proximity as these unexpressed emotions become stored. Later this latent energy appears in your body as a discomfort, ache, pain, or disease.

Do recognize that pain can be a blessing if you see the benefit it offers. Yes, that may sound strange, but what other indicator do you have in a world where so much of life is trapped within the mind? The mind and its trappings create a web of intrigue with its stories and dramas.

Ego will routinely take the opposite viewpoint to keep you as its host engaged, regardless of the position taken. Yes, the old fight or flight aspect of ego is launched. Truly it does not matter if the host lives or dies as long as ego has maintained the relevance of its rantings. Its ongoing purpose has now been newly satisfied. In this way, it can continue in the ravages it creates. It's not personal — it is as it is. So much so that life can be a torment and painful experience, as opposed to experiencing the joy and creative expanse intended for each Soul embodied here.

It is rather foolhardy to expect something so primal as ego to understand life from a more elevated stature. Thus, ego can take either side of an argument and never lacks an opinion or words. Ego's original purpose was to protect its host (you) while anticipating any occurrence that might endanger it.

Ego can be your worst companion or best friend. Best friend when you have something from which you need protection and worst companion most other times. So, being aware of the mental trappings that go on upstairs is most important as you become the monitor of the endless mental chatter that goes on there. In observing and not judging, see the folly of what is being bantered about.

It's quite entertaining when you look at ego in this way and do not give stock or weight to its many judgments. What does it matter how someone looks, or if their hair is just so? Is their talk meant to infringe on your rights, or are they only making small talk? The drama and storyline created in the mind are just that — a drama, a story. You do not even know if any of these assumptions are true. In most cases, they are not. They do create dramas that play on in the mind, though. The rambling dialog continues and seemingly never stops. This is where you become the guardian of what flows between your two ears. Monitor your thoughts. Are they uplifting or judgmental in nature? Know you are not to be the judge and jury for every occurrence that flashes before you. Surely your mission and role in this life is something of greater value than being the judge and jury for each activity you encounter. To what purpose and to whose benefit does placing judgment serve anyway?

Once you are more fully aware of such folly, you can become the Awareness and engage in the day in a more conscious way. It is this that leads you to know of the flow and how it does go.

Chapter 2

The Flow and How It Does Go

As you look at your current path, when you shift your focus and thoughts, you will change your attitude and demeanor. Do this first to move out of recurring negative ideas that might keep you trapped in a mental loop. This will allow you to see new choices with differing outcomes. So how do you enter the flow of Universal consciousness, and what will keep you there?

You will need to get out of the way of your own limitations to engage in this mighty river of life. Remove the mental blocks to what is going on around you in order to sustain and remain there — as you bring forward all you desire to manifest within this life.

Do you have a long-held dream or ambition that is waiting to be born? Can you bring it into your awareness now and allow it to be prominent in some way? Dreams are those things that make your heart sing and bring joy to your being. This is why you have come here ... to create, manifest, and share unique experiences.

So how is it (by entering into this flow) that you can also allow what is to be? It is by shifting out of your head and into your heart. It is to discover your heart's desire as it awaits manifestation. This thing you are to bring forward is your unique quality or gift. Only you have the ability and vision to bring it forth in your unique manner. It is what makes work play and becomes an extension of you as it resonates so deeply within. This gift yearns to break free from a self-made prison of limitation and lack. This is where it has been confined and restricted entrance into this world of form. In time, you are meant to experience your true expression, your purpose, and to manifest it into this reality. Discover what is awaiting its entrance into this world. It waits for your focused attention and the desire to physically bring it into being.

Enter into the energetic space where there is no start or finish. It is as it was yesterday and continues to be today. In the flow of consciousness, you do access a warehouse of measure that energetically holds all you might bring forth into this life so that you might experience ultimate happiness or mirth. Mirth in that happiness is sometimes fleeting, yet mirth is what resonates from a higher vibrational frequency. It allows a deep-seated contentedness to come forward and express itself into this world of form. A very similar yet different vibration to it is joy.

Enter into the flow of consciousness. You reside in the flow of Universal consciousness as you do those things that resonate with you and your Essence. But how do you get there? It is when you stay in a positive state of being. You will feel it in your heart and experience it through your actions, which we often refer to as *doings*. Know what you seek is attainable when you stay out of the negative *what ifs* mentally projected upon you. You can always listen to the banter of the mind and allow it to draw you down. Choose rather to shift into a *what is* thought instead. These thoughts will propel you into the flow of consciousness. It is really that easy. So when you have the option to think an uplifting thought or one that makes you feel sad or brings you less fulfillment, less joy, less laughter, choose the happier choice. Choose to think upon happier concepts, as you are the gatekeeper of all of your thoughts and feelings. Shut the door to those negative *what ifs* to allow other possibilities to enter in. Thoughts create feelings, and feelings create emotions. Emotions bring forth actions or reactions, and these result in your manifested reality.

Remember, though, it all begins with a single thought. Choose those things that bring a smile to your face and allow joy to enter your heart. Then you are on the path to getting into the flow. Once there, you will never want to leave this state of contentedness. It will draw you into other similar thoughts. Each will propel you a bit higher in vibrational bliss. One upon the other will build and draw you into something akin to a whirlwind. You are enveloped by a momentum that is limitless and unbounded. Know too, all is possible when operating from a state of surrender when you do not predetermine each outcome.

How can other possibilities reveal themselves to you when you have operated from a place of already knowing each thing? You have already determined how they will turn out. Can you really know with certainty any outcome? It is when you enter into a state of not knowing, a state of wonder, that other possibilities can then enter in too.

Contemplate and recognize you cannot know all. Seek for the unknown to become known to you through surrender. It is from this state of allowing that more can readily enter in. Allow for other outcomes to come into play. When all is already known, how can life's mystery enter in to surprise you?

So here is something you can do that has not yet been practiced but by a few. Sit with the intention to draw higher frequencies to you. What do we mean by this? Center yourself and recognize that all life, as is your being, is composed of atoms. Atoms can change their spin, their rotation when their frequency changes. When they are recalibrated in this manner, they can out-picture a different pattern than they held before.

So how do you change your frequency and what

can be done to elevate things in such a way that can also shift the rotational spin of an atom? It is the vibrational frequency that allows for this change to occur. By making slight modifications, these higher frequencies can be a part of your daily moment-to-moment life. Drawing forth higher frequencies is something that has been a part of mankind's earlier history yet has been lost for a time. So in reintroducing it, we seek your undivided attention and ask that you enter into this teaching when you are ready to access a more elevated state.

To elevate your frequency, let's do a little tune-up. Begin when you have quiet time to devote to this topic. In that way, you can experience the full measure of what is being conveyed … as it is distinct and unique to our discussion now.

Hold this in your mind's eye as you shift your focus to elevate your personal frequency. In doing so, you will simultaneously raise your consciousness. This shift will create a buoyancy that can be engaged even when you feel downtrodden.

Sit in a comfortable position and focus on the following lines. It is this mantra and the subsequent verses that will provide you with a geometric rhythm which will resonate within your being. In its repetition, your consciousness can be elevated and raised to a level that will allow you to outwit the mind in its unending banter.

These words will shut down its chatter by slowing the ramblings there. In this way, you can create a peace beyond human understanding as this creates an ebb and flow within you like no other. Focus, remain centered, and now begin —

Mantra and Verse

Om Bava Shanti (3x)
Shanti Allah Hum.

Om Bava Shanti (3x)
Shanti Allah Hum.

Always present, yet now so bright
the Flame within me does now ignite.

It is burning through my body this day,
and does race like a bonfire to clear away
all in discord, not aligned within,
does consume and expand as we begin.

Mantra and Verse
(continued)

Do know that Light and Love
do fill all vacuums and voids.

They do illuminate and grow,
eliminate what's buried below.

We now seek to remove that which hinders your life force,
to go and do and Be, of course.

So move this day, empowered, and know
that this breaks up, consumes what blocks your flow.

Now you are in the momentum of Love
as this resonates and restores your Essence
from below to above.

For you are more than a mere body, you see,
and as such, do command to now be set free.

It is in the repetition of these lines that a synergistic energy is created, and a raising or buoying of energy occurs. In this simple act of surrender to the words and their essence, much can be shifted and reengineered.

The components that have been given to restructure a life in need of assistance are miraculous. So many aspects within life are miracles in motion. Beginning with the movement of the sun and stars to the birth of a child, from creation and existence to seasonal cycles, all are miraculous in their core essence. Life is amazing. And to *not* recognize this and to *not* stay in a state of awe throughout the day is *not* entering into its sacredness. If you were to walk around and focus on the marvels that exist in nature, you would truly allow your body a reset of sorts. A chance to breathe and be present, rather than rushing through life as you race to the next activity. So pause as you stay conscious of your surroundings to more easily enter and thus tarry longer in Universal flow.

Chapter 3

How to Move in Concert with the Flow

The flow mentioned in the last chapter will bring you to that space where you will recognize choices that allow you to remain in the flow or know when you have moved outside of it. This moves us to the next facet of being, which is consciousness in flow.

It is always your choice to engage life at one level or another. It is not to say that one is higher or better, but when objectives can come to you at a faster, almost breakneck speed, wouldn't you prefer to be caught up in that energetic whirlwind? Wouldn't you prefer to undertake objectives that move you toward your purpose, sooner rather than later, and to do so in a healthy body while enjoying a happier state of mind?

We seek your wholeness, good health, and happiness. Thus, we provide a road map, so to speak, to guide you to a more expedient path leading to the destination you desire. A path will lead you to a road, which turns into a highway. All will get you to your destination, but the speed at which you travel and arrive is the difference you will experience. Why take the longer route when a highway of travel will get you where you desire to be so much faster?

So, being in the flow, as we have said, is a welcome space in which to be. Momentum is already a part of the flow that moves you, and so rather than you working, set Universe to work on fulfilling your objectives. You carve out what you want, outlining or perhaps detailing certain points for Universe to know. Universe then sets out to deliver more of your focused attention back to you. Will you be amazed when all, plus other unimagined aspects, are provided?

Begin by maintaining positive thoughts. When you engage in uplifted thoughts, those that make you happy, you will enter into the flow garnering momentum as you add purpose to the equation. This will transport a slow-moving scenario into one of high speed and staggeringly quick outcomes. These positive thoughts will keep you in this energetic whirlwind, some know as the vortex. It is a spectacular place to be, and we seek your alignment with Universe by employing this first activity: positive thought. This will allow you to go into this most preferred energetic space, maintain your ability to stay there longer while doing so with great ease.

Remain in the flow of consciousness. It need not be difficult. You do not need to be of a certain age to enter. Our desire is to relate this knowledge to those of any age who are young at heart. Forming early habits before the mind must be retrained would be the easiest. When you implement and strive to stay engaged in positive thinking throughout the day, the fruits produced will yield unexpected outcomes that will buoy up everything that follows such thinking. You are the creator of all things within your life. Thus, this will allow for unprecedented advancements to be experienced and for you to more readily enjoy the fruits of your creation. This is most critical to understand.

When you engage and practice this teaching, new opportunities can come to you at any age. Age is only a number and a state of mind. Know that if you choose, you can become ageless in these endeavors. Do not limit what you want to accomplish by a perceived number that has no real value, except to remind you that you have time yet to continue and achieve.

It is really about keeping track of what runs in your mind's eye and refocusing on better, more positive thoughts — if that is the current need. Redirect to positive ideas, ones that make you feel good. Perhaps the term happier thoughts is a better way to describe this. Engage with those things that produce good emotions and good feelings within you — especially as you are the best one to know if something resonates positively and appropriately within. Keep track of this and know that as soon as an idea shifts outside of what brings a smile to your face, then it is time to refocus your thoughts and ideas to another topic, or perhaps to slightly shift the way you perceive the idea.

Remember to have fun with your thoughts. Even the statement, *the devil is in the detail* (which it is), should be considered with mirth. Know when you place a weighty demand to do something exactly this or that way, you have limited its creation. Do not define everything so precisely. Allow for the sheer merriment of the moment to come forth in a joyous way. Do not limit or constrict how life is able to express itself to or through you or to regulate it in some way.

Enjoy each moment and allow for a little folly to exist in the mix of things. Shift the way you receive and perceive thoughts and ideas. Maybe make a game with whomever you share this teaching. Have fun with these words. When you stay in the flow of consciousness and remain centered in this whirlwind of sorts, you can move mountains of resistance and be in the space you seek so much faster than you thought humanly possible. You might test this out and see how much fun and amazingly effective this premise can be.

Chapter 4

No Opposition, Only Opportunity

The flow of consciousness is how you enable much within your life to unfold with ease and in a most effortless manner. When you surrender, you allow Universe to bring to you what awaits manifestation. It is in the state of *not* knowing, as we have said earlier, that new opportunities are released into your world. You will find new opportunities through the surrender component. Why is this so?

You may be content to express your life as your parents have dictated or perhaps as you believe life has demanded. These may not be those things you have been waiting to bring forward or give birth to, in a manner of speaking. In this way, you can get off-track from what you were destined to do or be. Sometimes life can take you on a ride. If, however, you seek another destiny, then something will present itself to shift you ever closer to the path that calls to you. The shifts will keep occurring until you arrive nearer to what you have wanted to out-picture in this lifetime. Might you reflect now upon what that might be?

What awaits is what you have already manifested, and it waits in the expectancy of its birth into this world of form. Let's discuss this. Your co-creations are all those things you create through your thoughts and associated choices. They may have nothing to do with your life work but are what you have brought forward through your thoughts and interpretations — your perceptions via the rose-colored glasses worn during life experiences you've had as this personality — in this lifetime. Although no experience is a mistake, steps can be made that take you away from the path you have chosen. But each step is valuable in that they will show you how certain steps are not preferred, redirecting you in some form or fashion.

What awaits is what you have already manifested ... alludes to something that was envisioned by you prior to embodying here. You also have previously created energetic gifts, termed tools within these writings, that are available and accessible from within your own personal warehouse — your own gift gallery, of sorts. But, too, you can also call upon what is universally accessible. And also, consider a vibration or frequency that allows access to other energetic treasures. These are accessible and attainable when there is a vibrational or energetic match to do so while physically placed.

Do you see when you are in a space of happiness and moving in Universal flow, you operate at a different vibrational frequency than when moving outside of it? When aligned vibrationally, all is accessible and available because you have tuned in to what is already yours to claim but remains slightly out of reach. Once you vibrationally synchronize or align to its frequency, then it can become accessible. This is the true measure of attunement and successfully reaching the measure that will bring you all you seek in this life in a most effortless way. You see, each thing has always been within reach. Access is available through your desire, intention, and focus.

Tune in now as you
embrace to fully recognize
all is energy, vibration, frequency

Your purpose is waiting in a full state of readiness and expectancy. Your anticipation of its arrival brings it into being when it becomes physical in your expectancy of it, through your thoughts and feelings. You feel it when you align with it vibrationally. It is there awaiting your alignment in a state of pure potentiality. Your thoughts and vibration align with it when you are in this state of true manifestation.

Now from this state of conscious creation, vision, and expectation, you can begin anew. Let us explain what we mean here. It is from a state of anticipation and expectancy that a vibrational component enters into the equation. There is a degree or frequency that is created during the creation process. So it is not the actual product being conceived but the vibration or the feeling component you sought to experience. It is attaching to and resonating with this vibrational component, which allows for the manifestation to be brought vibrationally into the physical realm.

It is from this state of expectation to allow what is to be. Not mentally knowing, but allowing from a state of surrender so that all might flow and fall into its aligned space. Perform your day with the belief that all you seek is already here, as you behold it inwardly, in its fully manifested form. No opposition — only opportunity exists here.

It is a miraculous and marvelous thing when all falls into place, and this does occur. You see, all must be aligned for this to happen. All of heaven lights up to the glory of this, for it is truly an amazing sight to behold ... when all components fall into place for such a manifestation to be made physical.

Chapter 5

We Seek and Find

As we move from this to that, from unconscious creation to consciously creating, let us pause for this understanding to become internalized into the inner core of your being.

It is often heard, but not fully understood, how this can be. So many lifestreams do not yet outwardly know what their purpose is and how to go about determining what it is. They seek to find it and begin in the doings of it before too much more time passes.

This is also referred to as your reason for being. How do you align to recognize and know what it is? Have you stayed centered now that you know how to get into the flow of consciousness — how to enter into the whirlwind of this synergistic flow, and how to stay there? Then, how to learn or seek to find that which has seemingly eluded you until now? What is it that makes your heart sing with joy and happiness as you enter into doing a task that leads you to the next one? In doing them, does joy spring up as these activities so resonate with you that you glow with happiness? Have you tried for a time to be — to simply be as you see what thoughts enter in?

Do you agree that sometimes you just have to slow down a bit and still your mind in order to see what is waiting around the next corner? Sometimes, busywork gets in the way. You must, from time to time, determine what is meaningful to do. And decide what is simply busywork that consumes your time without having much merit. For you do not see (in this moment) what is just beyond your grasp. All the doings or actions are not how you connect to that Part of you, which is aware of what you do not see right now. For you see, you cannot connect to that Part of you which has less connection with the doings but is all-expansive when you are Being.

Do you hear the small voice that offers insights and guidance? That is not ego ... it is surely something else. Observe this as you look within for a more deeply held understanding as you engage internal counsel. Did your parents or those who gave you early direction in life tell you to seek such inner awareness? So many answers do lie within.

Seek to still the mind by utilizing the verses provided earlier. Consider doing so again once all of its components are more fully understood. This process is yet another tool to add to your toolkit of awareness. Seek to access, employ, and mentally disengage in this way — routinely.

When you still the mind and look within, insights will most certainly appear. Don't look elsewhere, for you already have all the necessary components. As Dorothy found in *The Wizard of Oz*, she already had all she needed to get her to where she longed to be. She discovered she'd had this ability throughout her travels but didn't know it until she had taken many detours and laid claim to numerous adventures. In the end, Dorothy discovered she'd already possessed all she needed to return home.

Know that you would never have been left here stranded, so to speak, without all the necessary tools to allow for a successful, almost miraculous outcome. Manifest all you desire in this life. Many have become so distracted with trivial pursuits, such as looking youthful, materialism, and social media activities, in who is doing what — that no one is minding the storehouse of their own treasures. If you are always looking elsewhere, who is present to handle things on your homefront? Know that while this sort of connectedness is a remarkable thing, most things in excess tend to be a bit too much. When overindulgence is preferred, tarry in the arms of the Loving embrace Universal Love offers. It will indulge you in unbounded ways and is an excess that will *not* overwhelm or unbalance you. Satiate in this and perhaps *not* that.

Chapter 6

Love — the Underlying Key to It All

Might you consider now Universal Love as we contemplate its *Loving embrace*? Do you see how one thing does lead to the other? And so when you return to the earlier verses given, invoke and engage this Love. Let us tarry as we begin in a way of Loving measure as we move into Love's expansive and boundless portal that will always and unceasingly embrace, nurture, heal and restore.

So do recognize you have a Loving Aspect that wants your every success. Universe, God, Father, Mother are all terms for the Higher Source that seeks to offer direction and guidance. We recognize the term love is underutilized and not always connected to the unlimited potential of Universal Love. Engage now with its fuller measure to energetically evoke a vibrational frequency, unlike any other. Engage with this frequency in a more conscious way.

Love is indeed an emotion. But it is so much more than what most routinely associate with it. When its full efficacy is discovered upon the broader interpretation, it is consciously internalized and put into play. With this understanding, Love can become more expansive when you release its vast energy as you engage with it in this way. Call it into action within your world and into this physical octave with intention and purpose as you squarely place your focus upon utilizing it in its fuller measure and limitless potential.

What do we mean by this? Love has an energetic vibration that elevates and raises the vibratory frequency when it is consciously called into being. This activates its unique and expansive healing potential. When tapping into love this way, at this level, when you invoke this Love, it evokes an accelerated frequency.

So when you align with Love and the aspect of Love as you focus upon it now, rather than engaging its more common definition, you can enter into Love's all-encompassing vibration as your energy is buoyed into another vibrational frequency. If you have not felt this in the past, you might pause to feel this energy as you consciously invoke it now.

Your energy reacts to match its vibration, as will anything which comes into contact with it. As it moves out into the world of form, it will elevate the vibration of everything in its path before returning back to you.

Seek to no longer limit Love or simply equate it to a physical emotion — an emotion that defines a certain way to feel toward another person or thing. Recognize and now feel how Father and Mother Earth feel toward all of Earth's inhabitants, how the Angelic Kingdom feel toward humankind, how Beings of Light, Universe, God feel toward all creatures from all Kingdoms. By taking this one intentional step, a frequency is created that resonates differently. Tap into this frequency by consciously feeling their Love and focused devotion. Do so by coordinating your mind's eye with your heart center. Through this combined action, in time, you will feel the full efficacy and expansiveness of this Love.

It is from this perspective that you might now express this word and draw all of its kind back to you as it then moves out into the world. It is through the full circle approach of bringing back, complete unto you, what you have put forth as it increases accordingly. When you feel the effect of what you have introduced vibrationally, you will understand its limitless expanse.

This vibrational aspect has been readily accessible yet not often consciously employed in recent times. Now with this one added understanding, more is offered, and its true potential can be realized. Consciously utilize, engage, and invoke this concept of Love. See the results of this energy when purposefully introduced once again into the physical realm.

Expansive opportunities await as you recognize the ability to engage all of life and Universe from a different vantage. From this stance, you can move mountains within your world and thus reap any desired outcome more quickly than before.

All of life wants your success; wants you to have all you seek. Wants you to find what has remained hidden for a time, and with your continued focus, conscious Love, and devotion ... can you now see how all is truly possible?

Even the spin of an atom can be recalibrated when engaged to utilize a different vibrational frequency.

All is energy, vibration, frequency.

And so it is.

THE GREATER PURPOSE
Book Two: The Purpose Trilogy

The ORIGINAL
PURPOSE

Answers the Age-Old Question —
Why Am I Here?

Robyn G. Locke

GIVEN BY THE ELDERS

THE ORIGINAL PURPOSE

Table of Contents

Preamble

We know, oftentimes, that to move into uncharted waters is difficult and sometimes seems entered into with a degree of trepidation. Know that as we continue further, there may be steps within this process that uncover a pathway you are meant to become aware of in this lifetime today.

And so we do say to engage all from the measure of Love as this is the measure we seek to connect you with this day. For in this discovery and all that is to be given, know that above all else, you are deeply Loved. Universe, Source, all that elicits a posture of how you came to be here in this space in time, do continue to support you and each of your endeavors.

Always know this is the truth behind each measure, each step, each understanding that does evolve from this space (moving) forward. We give this as we move now to continue.

Preface

So often, in the formulation of life, there is not the full understanding of what coming to Earth, incarnating here and being a part of the flow of all that is in existence when one is physically placed. And so know that as you have chosen to reside in the consciousness and the densities of this Earth platform, you had made the election to do so. You had made the election because you wanted to understand something you could not (understand) in any other way. It was from this premise that the possibility and endless potential of what this Earth experience might express itself to be. It was this, then, that caused you to move into physical form and begin the rounds of incarnation here.

Often, there is not the full understanding of knowing that life flows differently here (on Earth) than when one is in spiritual flow. The densities here are expressed as they are for a unique purpose. And that unique purpose is so that you might more fully know how thus and such feels. For isn't it the feeling that gives you the understanding of the quality of what is or is not preferred?

We will say that there is an aspect that is not fully known when there is the posturing of preference to incarnate here. And by this we mean, that it is not fully understood, the full weightiness of what the uniqueness of this Earth plane does evoke and allow one to feel. And it is in the feeling component where so much more can be understood. So that when each lifetime is complete, there is an energetic accounting of what occurred.

The gifts, and those qualities which have been established to become known, are then uniquely those that are qualities imbued by the Soul Essence. And the Soul ultimately seeks for all of its known accomplishments, all of these known qualities, to be reabsorbed when the being that is incarnate recognizes that there are gifts to be claimed.

And the value to the being, or personality, or the one in existence to claim these things, is that they do not need to be, at this point, redeveloped. In other words, you do not need to do them all over again, for they are already the property and ownership of the Soul Essence. It is merely in the recognition that you seek to reintegrate that which is of its rightful owner. For you see, Soul Essence seeks the totality of the wholeness which it does seek to incorporate into its being and world.

And so when the incarnation is the last one, then there is the preference to draw all those gifts in so that the wholeness might become known. And the value for the personality or the one living the life, to claim those, does give a fuller measure of ability to the one who has not yet established the right to do so any other way.

Stepping into

Chapter 1

Transition

Do you recognize that often there are subtleties under-way and underfoot, subtleties that will lead you to the path of your preference or perhaps something else? We would say as you move, you do so with purpose. But when you move listlessly, or you move without a preferred agenda or objective in your future, then how do you move from here to there effectively?

And so we would say when one transitions, they move into an altered space. Altered in that it is not as it is when physically placed. We would say when one is physically placed, there is more of a definition of the time in space in which they reside ... physically.

As you move out of the body and into that transitory time, in between embodiments, there is not the anchoring one might feel while earthbound. And so, it is more of an illusionary premise. Although we would say when you are in that space, it does feel most vivid and real. And it does feel as if you know all that you need to know because in this space, you are anchored further with the understanding of what you knew before.

What you believed while physically placed is what you are reinforced with during this time. And so all the different perceptions you held while in the body are anchored and reinforced when out of the body. And so in this time and in this space, there is the illusionary premise that there is an all-knowingness in that existence.

And we will tell you this is illusionary because when you come from here to there, Earth to transition, you are reinforced by all you knew while physically placed. And so there is the aha moment that does transcend all time because, during this experience, you are anchored with what you knew to be true, thought to be true, believed to be true. And perhaps it was, or perhaps it was not.

And so we would say while feet are firmly planted on this Earth, to do all you can to enlist measures. And to do those things that will further reinforce a knowingness but not from the posture of the mind and not from the posture of ego.

For when the mind and ego lay siege on what must become known, and if there is a tinge of inner validation, an inner awareness that is not aligned as it might be when it is more placed toward egoic measure or mind stimulation, and not anchored initially from the heart and the heart center, then you may have an understanding that may be adrift of what truly is.

When you transition, you move into a space of being given reinforcement of what was believed before. In that space as one does move to progress and adopt what is to occur within a subsequent lifetime, there is not the questioning, there is not the wonderment, nor the understanding of what knowing something else might elicit.

And so we would say it does alter all that does pass and move beyond this time. For it is the structuring, and the planning, and the doing of the objective to prepare for the next step … to prepare for the next embodiment. To get all the ducks in a row, so to speak, so as you move to embody once again, you embody with a premise devised from this time.

And there may be individuals who energetically align and aspire to move into different arenas as well. And you and they do confer and are aligned to move an objective forward. Perhaps there is a belief that to experience this or that may yield a preferred understanding. But we would say that at this time, there is so much illusion in the midst of it all, that there is no longer the plotting and planning toward the original mission and toward the original objective. Although there is a component of one to the other, there is not the underlying and broad-based understanding that had come before.

With the original purpose, there is so much more that was comprised within that so that the fuller measure, the fuller understanding, the energetic component which comprised all these various nuances brought to a head. And so there is in many regards a minimization, a minimizing of what was understood, what might be understood, and what might be enacted.

And when one considers that many have lived from an oppressive state and are oppressed mentally, they then move into this transitory time and do not have the full scope of *all is possible*. There is a miniaturization and almost an inability to think from a grander regard. To move into more of a broad-based perspective of what might be understood were it to be deployed and employed.

In this transitory time, there is a moving from this to that, and then onto something else before the next embodiment is yet to occur. And so we would say to elicit questions during this time. Elicit multiple questions and ask for more to be given. Do not be directed so easily. For when one stops to inquire, when one stops to ask or elicit more, then there is the possibility for more to enter in.

We would say to linger in all regards. And to not move swiftly from here to there. And to pause. And to contemplate. And to move in less illusionary but more realistic terms by calling forth those who did reinforce your life while physically placed, for they are still accessible at this time. For in many regards, they are with you from lifetime to lifetime, and know your struggle, know your accomplishments, and know your objectives.

It is the disconnect from these ones, and the disconnect from the greater premise and greater purpose, that does often allow less to be known. And we seek for the maximization, for the full incorporation, for the alignment of the one to become known more fully. So then when they move, and they enlist to do more, they can do more from a broad-based perspective. They can do and accomplish more in a more uplifted manner. They can do and set about to set intentions so those who would buoy them up instead of envisioning something of a lower nature, hoping there would be a realization from that lower space to one of greater precipice.

And we would say it is the posturing and planning and doing so without enlisting guidance. For there is guidance, but you have greater guidance that is accessible, that is available, that is all about you even in this transitory time.

And so we would encourage one to the other, to move from the space of wanting to know more, wanting to enlist all the tools that are available. And those tools are available upon your call and your recognition of wanting more (and) of asking and enlisting assistance.

When this does happen, when there is the true calling forth of that which will enable you to know more, to do more, to be more in a subsequent time for the plotting and planning will be done in a more measured way, and will be done in a more uplifted way, and will be done in a way where there are dynamics brought into play that will be of a more significant nature.

For you see, many that are within the Earth premise today live meagerly and do not feel that there is the expanse within Universe to provide more. Do not feel the abundance from which Universe does exist and offer each within the round of incarnations. And so there is almost an aspect of not believing there is enough to go around.

And we tell you this is not so. And so when you are in that proposed arena, that area of illusionary wonder, remember this — remember when you ask, more is given. And when you call forth those who are Stewards of your lifestream, those who are Guardians of you, those who are watchers of what you are doing, they await your asking. They await your questioning. They await your wonderment of why they are there and that you even recognize that they are there. For often, they can be so close but yet so far away because there is not the recognition of who they are within the dynamic of the day.

When you move into a transitory position, remember, *if nothing else*, to ask that all be given that would move you back to your original purpose. Move you back to your original objective for embodying on this physical plane, on this Earth plane. By merely asking, you will open up a dynamic of what more might be given and known so these things exist with an understanding of all that might be. And that there might be a higher vibrational way to attune and to glean more from the existence from which they will soon be within.

And so we move to the next step, but we do want you to understand within this transitory time that there is much to be gleaned. There is much to be understood, but it is to be recognized that it is not as vivid and as actual as you may believe when in that space. For as we have said, it is an illusionary posture in that time and space.

If you will embrace that and know that it is a reinforcement of many things that are or are not so, then you will move into that space with a greater understanding and knowingness of what might be given, what might be offered, and how you might move into the next round of incarnation.

Behind the Scenes

In the backspace, in the backdrop, in the behind-the-scenes of activities that exist within your heritage, within the past that you intrinsically have known before, each pathway does elicit a purpose. For as you step into the knowingness and becoming the awareness of the purpose that you did initiate, that you did plant the earlier seeds to allow the growing and cultivation of the awareness of that activity or thing, it is more specifically the energy that you sought to understand. And in understanding the energetic component that was amiss and lacking from your current awareness, was to know more deeply how something felt.

And so that is the true navigator, do you see, within this life and any other. And even in the in-between state, there is always the movement. There is always the proclivity to understand and know something more deeply than could have been known without it.

And so during this in-between time, there is a request, a solicitation, a need to move from this space into the next. And we would say it is an ushering in of the elective process of moving to reincarnate yet again.

And we have said this is an illusionary time, for it is. For much is met in a way that is presupposed and allowed to occur in the existence of time, yet you might believe you have the option to move in one way or the other. And, of course, you do. But it is not seen as such, and it is more of a melding to move from one space to the next. To move into incarnation, once again, as if it were always presupposed, or already presupposed, that you would do so.

As you move to incarnate, there are those that come and ask for you to go about setting up your next life intention. There is an original intention that could be attached to here if it were known to be in existence. But at this point, there is not the awareness or understanding that the original purpose does exist.

And so there is more of an alignment with the premise that does surface at this point, which is a component of the greater, larger, more vast purpose. It is a component but not the entire understanding of what is. And so you move to embrace, understand, and add degrees of endeavor to it.

You add or facilitate that understanding in a greater way. And these others do come. So there is a community of sorts that are enlisted to facilitate what you could not perhaps do on your own. And these others are ready, and there are various levels of discussion to anticipate how one might meet and a feeling that is evoked. And an understanding that is given so more might be understood when you and they are physically placed. This occurs for a time, and they are enmeshed and melded into the fabric of the next life experience.

And so we will say there is the free will component, which is a part of this process and continues throughout each step, whether in the physical form or within the transitory one. For at each point, there is the opportunity to ask for more — to ask for a deeper understanding, to ask for more components, to ask for other players, to ask for something that resonates more deeply or is more purposeful. But oftentimes, this does not happen. And so the elements of this next life are given. And this process is moved through with a degree of not only specificity but a uniqueness and a clarity of choice.

As we look at this a bit more, let us say that there is not the engagement nor the willingness to shift from this to that. It is almost in the knowingness of what has come to pass, and what is lying at one's feet and what you are moving to enact, and do, and be in this next round, is more specifically understood.

And we ask if this is the purpose for which you understood? For there is an interpretation in this portion of the transitory time. An interpretation that all is known. But you see, all is not known. And only a component of what is known is actually utilized to put this next life plan into play.

We will say there is a compartmentalization. There is a limitation in that the understanding of what one is utilizing during this time is not as it is. It is not as the Soul Essence believes it to be. And so this is a degree of a limitation that is not recognized, not understood for the illusionary premise that is in play. And so oftentimes, there are components inserted and added that layer degrees of difficulty into the life path of the one who is to live this life in an uplifted sort of way.

For you see, when there is the need to make things a bit more difficult, to show how one can rise above the difficulty. How one can move beyond what is almost as if being in quicksand; there is not the ability to step up. There is not the need to move to this or that in a way that might be more uplifted, for there is almost a proving that one can access or reach a level that is most illusionary. For when one believes they have found it, they are ready to cast to the wind that which might propel them in a way that would allow them to navigate and reach their goal in a more illumined way.

So perhaps this is the area that is most foggy. For the premise it supposes is that all will be accomplished even with these added dynamics. But do you see when one has come from a difficult life and is heavy-laden, there is now the understanding that life is difficult and heavy-laden?

And so when the planning does occur again, there is the added layering which occurs that is most unnecessary. We share this component, so should you get to this space again, you choose differently. That through awareness now of that space, that you choose for it to be a more uplifted and easier next life, that you do not add in difficulty or some strategic move that would cause a layering aspect to be in play. Or more dramas to be undertaken. Or more scenarios to be engulfed by this one or that, that would delay, and insert so many different choices that it is most difficult to determine what one is to do at that crossroad.

So we ask for the next steps to be measured. We ask for consideration of the next steps to be, in a manner of speaking, simpler. And for more abundant-type scenarios to be introduced so the life isn't laden with lack, for there are many who know more lack than they do prosperity. And we seek to minimize this if nothing else. We seek to minimize this part of the equation so there is more beauty and light brought into this world, rather than the adversity that seems to be moving about this space today.

And so as there is the movement forward into the incarnation of the next life, various components are gathered and entered in. They are considerations, and they are contemplations, and they are activities and individuals who will line the way and be noted for what they interject into the next experience. And so all are a means of navigation. All are a means of a knowingness for which pathway to take when that person discussed a topic that has a recollection of memory that moves one to select this or that over another option.

Recognize each thing introduced does serve a purpose. And it is to connect the one with the other so a certain experience is rendered and felt.

In the In-Between Time

In the in-between time before the embodiment is known, whether it is the first, second, third, or some successive time in the future, there is the in-between time in which many do postulate and formulate what this existence is to be. And how it is. And what does occur when preparing for another round of incarnation, or perhaps the first incarnation.

We would say now, let us now focus on one who has embodied before and is in that in-between posture and moving to incarnate yet again. We would say within this time period, there is much activity. There is, of course, the reinforcement of all that has come before. So let us say all that you have known and believed in the life you have just left does remain firmly intact as the belief system that you carry forward into this next round. And this is the in-between, transitory state in which we discuss. What does occur in this platform of awareness?

When you step into this portal, you are then greeted by all you have known before or you feel energetically aligned to. And they do formulate and flow with you to reinforce the measures of understanding that were gleaned in the lifetime previously held. And so all does move in the manner of concurrence with what was and is within the belief system that grew from the awareness of the previous incarnation; all the platforms and understandings, as they were believed to have existed, now get that confirmation that they were as was believed.

We tell you that free will choice is a real thing. And when you freely choose to embrace this or that under-standing, it is not to be done lightly. It is to be done from the premise and the posture that this is a most important thing. And it is to be held in a most sacred way. For when you take on a belief, you do then limit the potentiality of any other belief that is in concurrence or opposition to the belief held.

For you see, when the belief is adopted, it has certain tenants or understandings that allow it to postulate and formulate as it might. And so we will say to look upon beliefs in a most serious way. For in that, you recognize how all that might be chosen, was not. For this one thing was what rose to the surface. And so to cast it aside in this in-between, transitory time would not be of the posture that Universe, Source Energy, would enlist. For to do so would be, in a manner of speaking, diminishing the free will component that led you there. And so why would Universe, Source Energy, or that Greater Power, seek to diminish what you have chosen to embrace, accept ... believe?

And so in this in-between time, when beliefs are held as they are, there is then that reinforcement of the belief. The belief then is held to the higher calibre and the higher stan-dard of equality and the equation that you have attributed to it. And so others come to reinforce that, and these beliefs are seen to be validated. But we will say, as we have said before, that this is an illusionary time. And so what you believe to be firmly affixed, firmly in place, may not be that way at all.

For Universe always seeks to make you correct in all that you postulate upon. And so when you look for confirmation of this or that, and you receive what you believe to be a sign that this or that is as you believed it to be, then you move on as you accept what is. But we would say to linger upon the premise. To linger upon the premise and to look beyond the limitation of the mind and the limitation of the egoic stance, which likes the confirmation and the validity of the rightness of choice.

And so there is a discernment that is underfoot, we would say. There is a discernment that is most necessary for you to … see. And that is the mind, ego, that chatter that goes on incessantly does seek confirmation of what it needs to know. But have you then ever considered to take what you postulate upon and muse upon it? Contemplate upon it in meditation. For it is in the contemplative moments when the small voice, the meek and mild voice, the voice that is not reactionary but does move to support, but in a more long-term sort of way. Not in the reactionary way that ego might employ. And so, might you look again? Look again at all the choices, all the belief systems, or perhaps the most important ones as the others will rise to the surface in their appropriate time.

In this transitory time, there is then the posturing of the beliefs, the buoying up of them, and those that are sent or that arrive as a means of confirmation of all that has been contemplated on before. And so then one does move to structure out the next lifetime. And the next lifetime may be in a few short years or maybe in decades or beyond. It is the preference, and perhaps, too, it is sometimes the posturing of the enlightenment of the one who does make the preference from a more quizzical standpoint of wanting to know more of what is.

We will say that to engage in what is believed to be truth and a validation of such, it is also the means by which so much more can become known. For here, too, there is an allowing, of asking — of asking to discover what more might be given. But you see, if you believe you already know, then there is no point to ask, for the reinforcements are all you sought in the first place. For with the reinforcements is the validation of the belief system that was in existence before.

And so we would say to stop and pause and to elicit to discover more. To call upon Angels, Light Bearers, and those whom you believe worked with you in the Earth plane to now step forward. To assist you in the path that you are moving to engage with once again. And so, seek to call in the reinforcements. Seek to call in those that worked behind-the-scenes while you were physically placed and ask for their intercession. Ask for them to interject into what might be moving forward.

For this is, as we might posture, an illusionary time, but it does not feel that way when in the throws of this most transient time. And so, as you move to do this or that, more is given. You perhaps preface what you would like to understand and know; know that you are moving from the reality from which you did exist before.

In other words, all is not known at this time. And you are not moving with a greater more-expanded awareness to plot and plan your next step. So as you chose to believe within the Earth quadrant, while physically placed, that same belief system has now moved with you from that existence to the next. And so they (your beliefs) are concurrently traveling with you. They are moving from the physical space to the non-physical space. And there is an almost seamless manner in which this or that is understood as it was understood before. And so there is not the ability to miss a beat. The confirmation is there; the ability to understand and discern what was gleaned before is most certainly the correct posture. And so now you move forward to make that life election in the next incarnation.

And perhaps you are in the posture that you do not believe in reincarnation. It does not resonate for you, and you do not understand how this can be when you know nothing else but this lifetime, as you have lived much of your life mentally. And we would say to move beyond the mental box. We would say to shelf the mind for a time and to recognize that the mental posturings will not get you from here to there. For now (in this space), you do not have the mental box that plays incessantly and the egoic measure that played when physically placed. But now you have simply the knowingness of all you knew before and what is.

Chapter 2

Uncharted Waters

As we begin this next chapter, know we move into uncharted waters, uncharted and unseen for a time. But might you consider that now is the time to move into spaces that were previously unknown? If you continue to simply regurgitate teachings that have been written and rewritten, said and re-said, tried and inspired to achieve a different outcome from a limited set of understandings … well then, you will not progress much further than you have before. But we would say it is time to move in a way that is now inspired to lift up and progress you beyond the current point in which you now reside.

Will you begin by taking deep breaths? In and out. With a purposeful intention to be able to incorporate and integrate that which we share. For in this way, you might be able to ponder upon the words that are given in the Love in which they are instilled and inspired to be conveyed, for we do share this and all information with a

Loving intent. A Loving intent that you may know more today than yesterday.

As life moves as it does, know there are postures and premises in play that are within the flow and the mix of the day. And by this we mean that they are crafted and energetically inspired by what is floating and wafting about. And so when there is, and are, postures that are of not the highest frequency, that are of not the highest nature that they might otherwise be inspired from, conspired with, that they might be otherwise attained, the day then shifts to mirror the energy which has collectively accrued.

And so, oftentimes, it is not that there is a pathway set out in stone that these things must occur in thus and such of a manner, but rather it is the choices made by those who are in this Earth embodiment that are there and collectively conspiring to create an energy that allows the movement to proceed as it is aligned to do.

And so we will say if there is a posture that causes the derailing of a more uplifted energy, that causes the breaking down of something that could be buoyed up by the energy that would change almost instantaneously were that different energy to occur, then there is a collective understanding that has drawn a different scenario into play.

It is not that there is an aligned measure to bring forward something that is not preferred into being from a universal posture, but rather the collective energies that are put into play by the ones who are physically placed. And those then do craft what moves forward into their future. Do you see it can be no other way?

Do you see that were there to be an inspired creation that was of a lower nature, we would say, why would Universe create such a pathway for those whom Universe so deeply Loves and wants only the highest and best calling; only the highest and best measure to be enacted within their day?

We would say that the energy created within the mix of the day from those who are aligned to create that energy, they then move that energy out and into being in a way only they can do. Only they then can move this energy to be one way or the other by the thoughts they keep. By the way they align their actions, by the way they instill their activities, and the way they forecast and project what they wish to occur within their being and world and future.

And so, know that each are the creator of their own destiny. And oftentimes, they know it not. For many do not see the fearful enterprise they might hold within a day, or the anxiousness, or perhaps even to say neediness necessitated by one's mental posture, does relegate what does move forward into their future reality. And so it is not that Universe has crafted life to be this way or that way, one way or the other, but rather it is the flow of energy that is created from the one who is postured in the Earth plane at this point in time.

When there is the posturing and the aligning with the negative aspect that is perhaps there but need not be. Need not be fully focused upon or given fuel to accelerate that which could be easily diminished by a different thought, by a different premise, by a different out-picturing, or promise for the day to unfold in a different way. And so we will say that there is not the need for certain things to come to pass, but yet they will most certainly be because that is the focus, that is the energy, that is the direction that is placed upon the activity that is now arising. Arising, one might say, from the ashes as the phoenix.

Arising in the beauty and light of taking something that is mired and not worth bringing forward, and instead bringing forward something of beauty, and light, and purpose. And so it is all how you see things. It is all how you intend for your manifestation, of what you mentally create, to move forward.

But do you see if you were to align and bring forward from the heart center, from that space once anchored and aligned in a more uplifted way, then all the energy and aspirational objectives would be brought forward in a more uplifted and inspired way? Then more might progress in a way that would germinate and generate something of value and of purpose, and aligned in a way that would move not only self but others to a different space at this point in time.

And so release these negative, not wanted feeling energy aspects, and move to align with those things that feel better. Move to align with each of these things in a way that will then uplift your next step. Will move you to be in a space of Love, and purpose, and understanding.

Can you see this is the better option? This is the better way to progress. For then, others can feel your energy, feel your optimism, feel your uplifted beat and measure. And they then can move to resonate like that rather than this.

We ask for you to consider this objective, this day. To move, and shift, and become all that you seek to be inspired from another. For you are to become the inspiration. You are to be the one who does inspire others who seek to emulate what you do, how you have gotten to where you are. And they, then, would like to shift and change into that. And it is all possible by merely redirecting the thoughts and the energy that you keep.

If you will do this one measure, so much more can flow into being this day. And in this way, we do set the anchor. We do set the foundational premise. We do set all we know into motion for the positivity you will evoke and give to mankind with this one undertaking when anchored in Love.

Align, Move Forward and Into Being

As we progress, let us look at the actual entrance into this world of form. Might you know all that does progress from this space is of measure? It is of measure in that it is to enact that one thing which you have presupposed to be the thing that will bring you into alignment with all that is.

And so as you move into Earth, you enter with a wonderment and awe of all that is to befall you; all that is to move into the line of space that is to connect each thing suggested and introduced in this transitory time that you have just passed from. And so this is a passing into the physical stage.

And within this physical time, there is a brief remembering, and then that does fade as well. It is during this time that so much now is being moved into cue, moved into action, moved into the alignment that will direct and allow your steps to be more purposely placed.

But during this time, there is also that forgetfulness that does enter in. Forgetfulness that has been enacted so there is a full understanding from the perspective of free will, and the occurrences of free will that are, in this way, allowed. For with free will, there is so much more to enter in.

But do you see from the transitory time where there was not the recall, there was not the full understanding of the true intent, the true purpose, the true understanding that much has been amiss for a time? It is amiss in that we suggest that there is not the full awareness in the transitory time. And so there is less than that moving into this space.

And so, without the full recall in the transitory time and moving into this space, there is then a lesser-than understanding of what is underfoot. And there is not the full awareness of what is being enacted and what is to be enacted, for there is not the full recall of the full extent of all that was put into play.

And so we suggest now there is not the awareness, not the understanding, not the full jettison of all that might be were you to be in this space from the original incarnation. For that is the closest you will have been in the full alignment of all that might be to enact this more relevant understanding moving forward.

And so what might be done? What might be done when one enters into a life form, and you must now rediscover the things you knew before? And in the rediscovery, there is, in many ways, the feeling that when you connect to that thing that perhaps is not even the aspect that is the truth component that you have discovered before. When you find that once again, there is a familiar feel, there is an aha moment that you have aligned with that thing you've been in search of for so very long.

But when the aha moment is not what it was meant to elicit, was not the full extent of understanding you were meant to glean, was not all it might have been once before, when that is rediscovered, and you believe you have now found that thing which was most prevalent, well then, what has it moved you to believe?

And we suggest it has moved you to believe something that was less-than, something that was not quite it, and now you have nestled into that premise, that concept, that belief pattern once again.

And so, how to shake that? How to shake that thing which is so seemingly important now? And we would say to do a subconscious reset where you release and relinquish so many things that are burdensome and are not as they were meant to be intrinsically understood.

We say to release them through this process so you might move differently. So you might embrace things from a higher calibre, a different calibre, a calibre more aligned with where you sought to be in this embodiment, where you sought to be in this way, where you sought to know and understand … more.

For you see, you came to understand how in this physical plane you would feel when enacting this thing that you did not fully understand. And so might you relinquish all you believe this day, all you have used as your foundational footing as that understanding that is all about knowing what might be in a space of not knowing? And so enlist now to not know once again.

Enlist now to know something more deeply, more fully, more completely in the space where you now reside. Do so by resetting the subconscious, doing the self-guided meditation where you release beliefs, doing some process that you will let your entire being know that it is time to shake it up. To shake it up and to allow more to become known by you. More to become known in that it is time to un-know what you think you may know. It is as simple as that.

It is allowing from the space of not predetermining what each thing might be, what it might mean, what it is, from a pure premise of allowing more to be in existence this day. Allow more to be in existence this day as you move to yield what you do not presuppose to know by relinquishing and releasing all that is in current play.

Do you see it is a shaking up? It is a reposturing. It is an allowing for the alignment to be held, and done, and occur differently. It is the pure potentiality of allowing more to be known, to eradicate and erase those things that have come before. Those things that have seemingly taken you off target. Those things that have taken you on a joy ride, so to speak. But sometimes, it is not in a joyous manner. Sometimes it is in a more beleaguered, and belabored, and problematic way. Because the mind does twist, and turn, and postulate, and formulate all that has come before. And the subconscious does store much of this within its groove, within its un-forgetting, unrelenting posture to protect. Do you see that oftentimes that which you believe to be familiar and feels right is something that is from a collective way, something you have carried with you for a time, and another time, and more time?

And now we say to shake the dust from your feet. To shake the lingering inability to connect as before. We say to reposture, reformulate, and look again with refreshed eyes. To see things from a manner of knowing there is more. Knowing there is more awaiting your fresh eyes to look upon it all again.

Do so this day. Reset the subconscious. Reformulate, look again, and reposture. Do so with refreshed and renewed eyes. Do so from a revitalized perspective. Do so as in the wonderment of the child. Do so looking upon each thing as you might with those fresh eyes that do not see what was before them, before.

Now look upon each thing and recognize that it was there for a purpose, but it was a bit askew. It was a bit adjacent to rather than in alignment with what you sought. And so when it was adjacent, and you drifted in that direction, you moved away from that which needed to be aligned with. And we just seek to move you back on course. To move you back to that point where more can transpire. And in that transgression of transgression-airy posture, and in that mode of moving, and transpiring from this to that, and aligning differently, you can then move in a way that does result as you prefer.

And so we ask this day for you to align as never before. To shift and move and to allow this reset of the subconscious to shift-change you. To move you to want to enact life differently. To allow things to drop from you, premises, or predispositions that are no longer necessary. And that now when you move, you will do so in a cleaner, clearer, less-encumbered way — a less-encumbered state of mind, a less-encumbered formulation of flow.

This is what we wanted you to know. That this is an important step. This is most diligently sought. And we seek for you to know it, to do it, and to align this way as never before.

Chapter 3

Your Earthbound Adventure

As we begin, consider this. Consider the vastness of all that is, and how it has come together, all these things to progress from this space, from this Earth plane. To have all the tools, all the necessities, all the things that necessitate a successful outcome of this earthbound adventure.

And if you recognize that there is no time in that space from which you came. And that time is illusionary and is felt here so uniquely. Then do you recognize how each thing is as it is for a purpose? That you have this opportunity to feel, and to do, and to experience that which you did not know before becoming earthbound. That which you did not know before entering this Earth plane. And so you have a true connectedness in all that is from the posture and the premise that these things were unknown previously.

They may have been supposed or believed to be a certain way, but there was not the actual understanding of it, fully, until there was an entrance into this dimension. And so we would say that this dimension is uniquely, aspirationally, intentionally, as it is, so that there is the full weightiness, there is the full understanding, there is the full proclivity to know that which was unknown before.

And so even in the drama of it, even in the midst of being amid all that is, there is, we will say, a beauty in it. For it is uniquely yours and uniquely an experience which will be intrinsic to your Soul's understanding of all that is. All that is before you now. And all that is in play.

If you look at this as your Soul might, for this unique experience and how this personality does walk this Earth, does take form, human form, in order to experience what is in this dimensionality of life. And so, do recognize there is an intrinsic gift and value given to the Soul experience that you experience. But there are some that have been in this platform, and in this performance, and in this game, in this reality for quite some time.

And we would say there is a lessening and the illusion becomes more permanently felt, but we would say this is illusionary also. But when you are in the midst of it all, when you are in the drama of it all, when you are in the throws of all that is, there is the firmly felt belief that this is real. And it is not. It is that which it is, but it is not permanent, and there is no permanence to it.

Each knows they will pass from the screen of life in a

time they are unaware of, whether by illness or another intent of the drama of the activity of this, which we will call your life. And know when it is time to progress from here to there, there will be an occurrence that will take one from here to there. And so do not get stuck in the midst of the muck of the day.

Do not get stuck in all that is, that does out-picture itself, for at some point you must buoy yourself beyond all that does out-picture itself in a most significant way here. And so we will say to align in the premise that you are a visitor from afar and you want to experience and know how this or that feels.

And when you have gotten to that understanding, and you know exactly how it feels, and you say this does not feel good, or it does not feel as I would prefer it to feel, or have assumed it to feel, or had laid claim to the belief of how this or that felt, but now I know more personally that it is not something I wish to experience, but I wish to experience the full totality of what lay in its converse. Then, you move with more purpose to enact that thing because you know what it is not. And now you move toward what it is. And what might be experienced and the expansiveness that exists there. Do you see this? Do you recognize there is more for you to align, and do, and be?

So shake off the dust from your clothing. Shake off the unreality which has layered and lofted about you. And that you move in step to all that does wait illumination. Does wait to be out-pictured and seen from the expansiveness where it lay dormant in waiting.

And we will say each thing is just within reach, just within your grasp. And so we ask now for you to remove the mental limitation. Remove that mental box of know-ingness. And do see how you can now place it on the shelf, for a time, as we discourse further. For there is much which we wish to share, but we will limit and share small kernels that are more palatable at this point.

And so as man came into form, and as man progressed in time, the diminishment of all that is known evaporated just a bit. Evaporated and was not as prevalently under-stood as before. And we would say that there is the procliv-ity, there is the understanding, there is the lack thereof, of so many small details that have become eclipsed. Those that have been minimized and eradicated, erased, removed, for they are not seen.

And when something is not seen, it is unknown until there is the pausing and the formulation for what was ... not; to be moved into place, and into experiential aspects of being, when one does focus and draw that which is submerged, so to speak, and below the surface.

We seek for you to do just that. For you to focus upon what is not seen, not known, not recognized, except for the feeling component that you can lay claim to. That you can pause, and meditate, or consciously envision what is not yet known for your lifestream.

As you pause in meditation, or in a meditational way, you can pull up those aspects that are just below the surface that are unseen at this time, but that await entry. You can draw forth energetic gifts that are yours to lay claim to from other undertakings in other times. You can draw these into your awareness this day. You can take in and understand all that does wait to express itself from a component of wonderment and awe. It is in the imagination that many (of these) can be assessed and accessed.

Do pause the mental gravity of the moment. Do pause the mental wonderment and exploratory nature of wanting to so define what will be said and move it off and away from further examination. Lay claim to more. Lay claim to more that is and awaits discovery now.

For we will say that when you pause, you might also elicit a posture through perhaps a small verse that does in rhythm and flow, allow you to engage because it will be a key of sorts. And you can take this and utilize it word for word. Or you can customize it as it does shift and change energetically with the insertion of other words, which may slightly change its rhythm and flow, but will work more intrinsically for you than this entry verse may in time.

And we would say it will go like this …

Shift-Change Verse

We seek for you to discover and find
what is key to discern and define.
Know through Light and Love,
    all things can flow from up above.
Encircle your life force with only those things
    designed to reinforce.

You see, you are all you need to be
    within this vast Earth density.
But as your true purpose awaits discovery,
    seek a means of rapid recovery.
It is why you came here; it is why you remain here.
So enlist a means of connection in this time.

You knew it originally for you sought it to be
    because you wanted to understand something more
    vividly.
But you needed this density, and it's become quite clear
    that it's time to enact what has always remained near.

Shift-Change Verse

(continued)

And so begin from the heart center, start from this space.
Begin in this way to facilitate haste.
Access this most valued resource to navigate a new course,
    so all might become known and engaged.

For over time it was lost, not seen for you see,
    when you cannot see something so vividly.
It's hard to recall, hard to know why you want it at all,
    but it was the means to understand more over time.

And so know now this as you seek to uncover each veiled gift,
    and the messages they sought to impart.
Start in Light and Love this day, to engage and put into play,
    what you seek in an unending way.

When you engage as suggested, consciously moving into cue,
    all you sought to behold for it was then you knew,
    by keeping mental thoughts at bay, throughout the day,
    all could be enacted in a most expeditious way.

How to Customize Your Verse —

Discovery of what you seek is the key,
so reframe each verse to shift in time
based on your mastery.

Free the little small voice who awaits and wants to say
how each thing can align in a most magical way.

Keep the beat and rhythm,
so you might align with what's best
to move forward over time to engage all the rest.

Enlist a moving connection, and this is key,
for all that's in play to now formulate and be.

Chapter 4

Your Original Incarnation &
Its Original Purpose

To consider life to be anything other than what it is — the magnificent marvel of all that might be created and made manifest — would be to diminish that which is. For you see, so much is determined by what the mind will allow to come through the portal, and pathway, and entrance into this world of form.

And so you see, often, there is a picking and choosing of what might be best to formulate upon. And we would say that this is a most weighty matter, for there is much speculation and disagreement as to why thus and such is so. And we will say that it could be because of your upbringing. It could be because of genetics. It could be for a myriad of reasons, but we would say you must ultimately take control of the mental vessel so you can move in a proximity, and a pathway, of the things you preferred to discover once long ago.

And there are many that are in embodiment who have been doing just that — embodying — for quite some time. And those we have reached out to in numerous platforms and methodologies to enlist that they then remember. That they remember what they set about to understand so long ago.

And so we will say this chapter deals with your original purpose. That purpose you crafted when you first took embodiment into form so you might understand, in an energetic way, how this or that would feel rather than as it might be in textbook or in a textbook-like understanding.

For you see, so often there is the posturing and belief of this or that, and Earth has been and will remain for a time a schoolroom of sorts, where one can step into form to understand more fully what this or that might truly be. And how it might feel to enact this or that, or to create and to emblazon some understanding, and how it would feel from the accomplishment of the undertaking, and the recognition of all that is set into motion from the posture of doing.

And some may believe this purpose is a thing, but really the thing is the byproduct of that which you energetically strive to understand. If you look at it that you can create and do most anything when you have the wonderment of all that is, and no restriction from the mind placed upon you, then you can see so much more can flow into formation. And then it is no longer in flux and flow but actually affixed and made more real by the enactment of it.

And so, move this day to understand what that purpose was so long ago. And we will say that in the in-between time and in subsequent embodiments, there have been life purposes for those incarnations. But we will also say that they are not the full expansive preference to know, do, or be in those subsequent times.

For each time the transitory time did take place, there was a degree of stepping down from that overarching premise that was first crafted. For how can it be that you would know as much from one embodiment to the next? And perhaps there is a greater understanding in one or a lesser understanding. But each one, as you moved into that in-between time, did reflect the understanding that was held when last embodied.

When that life plan was crafted and made for the subsequent incarnation, there was the understanding as it related to that specific life. For in that life, there may have been a buoying up, or not, of that being. And so if there was a successful encounter in that lifetime and there was more that was understood and gleaned, then the subsequent incarnation did reflect that, for there was more crafted perhaps into what was sought to be understood. But we would say that the overall understanding of what was wanted was not the full understanding of what was initially conceived.

Recognize this and know each thing is as it is meant to be. And because we have also shared that there are dual lifetimes in play today, dueling for supremacy and to achieve the outcome, perhaps, more quickly — but also, perhaps, more in tune with what is, then we will say there is another component at play here.

And so will you be receptive to receive that there is another dimension where it is almost a mirroring aspect where other lifetimes are also enacted? Where other realities are in play because other choices exist where another outcome may be perceived or wanted, for they are unique and separate occurrences and not exact mirror replicas of one to the other.

So there may be a completely different dimension going on concurrently with many of the same players to see the outcome that is derived in that understanding. And so this is a stretch of the imagination. This is a stretch of the understanding which may be in play within your own dynamic. But we would say to consider this as well, for it does have an overarching contribution to the mix that is in play today.

And so when you are in meditation, might you consider to connect to this parallel adventure? If you will do so, then you can see and feel if you are buoyed up, or not, in this other existence. And if there is a buoying up, might you consider tethering this existence to that one? So that if there is a means of reinforcement, if there is a means of advancement, if there is a means of drawing the energy from one to the other because you have wanted it to be so by your focused intention and your attention to it, then you can redirect some of that energy to you now.

We do want you to pause and to sit with this for a time. So that you might draw in that which you perceive, that which you now consider, and that which now is in play.

∽ Contemplative Pause ∽

And now that you have played in the energy that we have introduced, we ask you to continue to explore and to return often. And maybe refresh these words so that they might become renewed with you.

And you might say, *perhaps I am the one that others prefer to tarry with and tether to.* And this may be so. Then it is up to you to seek to connect with them. And you can do so by stilling the mind and allowing what may enter into it as you look at the vistas that are before you. Do you see one that is struggling, that seeks to connect with you, or unknowingly exists without the understanding of the tethering process? And so is it worthwhile then for you to seek the connection? And we would say, yes, because this is an aspect of your Soul and ultimately of you.

As you look upon life this day, do see it in a uniquely marvelous way. Because there are things you may not have known about before, yet have always existed. And so can you see when you tether and fortify another, you then buoy yourself up to a degree? Because you have enlisted steps to help another. And in that assistance, you can be so much more because now you are a lifeline to the other. And you will reinforce, and engage, and be able to bring forward that which may not have reached the level that you now exist in. And so, look at life in its wonderment. Look at life and the opportunities you represent, and that you have become aware of, so that you might be more in all that you do, all that you enact, and all today you know to be.

Chapter 5

Now That You Know

Now that you know, do you see how so much more is and does exist within life? Within the totality of all that you might do and be, do you see that as you seek more, more is given? As you yearn for an understanding and saw negativity and things that were not preferred in your past, can you look again? Can you look again and see the gift that was given? If not then, perhaps now? For in the recognition of the gift that had been there all along, you then look upon life in its totality in a different way. You look seeking to know what the gift is. You look in wonderment and awe, and with the quizzical nature of the child. Do you see that this is, as it is, for a purpose?

For if you readily saw each, then there would not be the mystery attached to the gift. And isn't the gift a bit mysterious when it is wrapped and disguised so that the full extent of what is inside that wrapped gift is not immediately known?

Can you look at life in this way? Can you look at life in the wonderment of all that it is? Can you see life exudes, and portrays, and emits almost an energy of wonderment, of possibility, of all that seeks to become known in the portal and the pathway that you've created?

The portal is the opening and the opportunity to see what was not seen. And the pathway is the means by which you travel to get to where you seek to go. And when you know each thing given does hold a key, a key to what you could not see without its added measure, then you look upon this gift differently.

You look upon it when you are ready to do so, with a bit of quizzical wonderment. And we have said it is the wonderment of a child. And so when you look, always knowing that life would never serve you that which is not for your betterment; is not for your discovery of knowing what it is, and then being able to implement it once the awareness has entered in. For you see, if you remain in the neediness and the less-than energy, you may never connect to the other.

And so know that this day: that the gift is truly a gift. And it is all that it needs to be, and it is in the awareness and recognition of what it is and needs to be seen to be, by you, for you to advance, in a manner of speaking, to the next level of play. And so know this as we proceed.

Gifts Given

And so, gifts present themselves in a variety of ways. And you may not see them as a gift. But know they exist in this guise nonetheless. If you have a course correction, if you have perhaps a calamity or some other issue has caused you to be and become perplexed, can you pause and look at it differently?

We would say when you still the mind and look from the quizzical aspect of a child, you can see what is more clearly before you and what has truly been given. It is another opportunity to see life in a different way. And so when you posture and determine that you want to see life differently, and you are willing to relinquish the belief system that you have held, then you can adopt and even adapt to new opportunities and things which were always present, yet presently unknown.

And these are nothing new. They have been invoked and utilized in previous times, but they are remaining dormant at this time. And if there are some who have discovered their methodology, then perhaps they might listen in, too, to see if they might expand what they know.

And so, you can formulate, and postulate, and imagine a variety of things. And each of those things have the potentiality to become real, to become known, to become a part of your day and put into play.

When you envision them, focus upon them for a time

and then release them to only reengage them later to stir them up, so to speak. To revive what you have planted as a seed. It is as if you were watering what you had planted. And so look upon each thing as the gift that it is. Look upon each thing when you move out of the angst of the mind, or the perplexities of the situation, to engage and to think of it once again, in a new way; in a way in which you might not have considered before.

Today, let us talk briefly about something that is perhaps new on the horizon, and, perhaps not. But it is how to posture and formulate more. And so when you consider that you have a hearing disability or perhaps a ringing in the ear, do you stop and say, *Hmm? What has caused this nuance? Why is this at my door?* If, however, you engage with this new addition to your life in fear, anxiety, and a bit of mayhem, that (mayhem) might develop in time.

For you see, when mayhem is introduced, or thought about, or there are perplexities that are felt, then you are not seeking a true resolve to the situation. But, rather, something that might be medically induced to subside the symptoms. But the symptoms are simply there to let you know that you need to look into this or that in a most whimsical way.

And so this day, there was such an occurrence. And the thought was at that point, *Hmm ... am I to look differently at this ringing in my ear? Why is this happening? And what might I do to alleviate it? Might I search for something that will allow me to hear insights and messages, perhaps, differently than I had before?* And that was exactly the right posture to engage and perceive.

And so do you see when you look at each (occurrence or situation) with a quizzical understanding, a quizzical way, a quizzical mental engagement, then you do not engage the fear aspect but the whimsy and wonderment of the child. And so, yes, there are other ways to engage that which seeks to share insights from another dimension. And oftentimes it introduces itself and sounds very much as the mental mind does. And so there is a degree of discernment which must be maintained, at all times, so that ego does not enter in and take you off-course.

And this can be rather perplexing over time when you begin to question each and every new insight because it is new. And it is not something that you've heard before. And how do you know if it is true, or not, unless you delve within and sit with it in contemplation, to know if this or that is correct or true? And so if there is another means where you can, almost like an on-off switch, turn on a means to (almost) hear the messages a bit differently.

We would say that you must resonate with what is given so you have that inner discernment to know if it is true. But we will also say there is a degree of distinction that can also be given so that you can determine what is what, and who is who.

And so this is what we seek to engage you with this day so that you might have more ingredients to put into the mix and that might make things a little bit easier to digest. As you look to understand and discern this insight, seek to still your mind once again, and then we will … continue.

∽ Meditational Pause ∽

And so we seek now for you to become and be, all that you might be. When insights present themselves that do not align with you as you might anticipate, sit with the premise for a time so that it might integrate, and you might receive it differently. These are signs and ways for you to look upon life so that not only might you integrate, but you may not, at this point, miss the greater objective. And the greater objective is to align you with all you seek, move you into that space of readiness, and to adopt then a posture that will move you to all that is.

For there is much that awaits your discovery and much that will move you — differently. Differently than you have moved in this lifetime, perhaps, but not in previous ones. For you have soared to great heights and done things unimaginable in the densities which exist here.

For from here to there, there is a great gulf, and this is maya and illusion. And the illusionary posture from which you now reside seems most dense, heavy, weighted as you fully feel this life experience, which is how it is meant to be. For you to not want an experience which is unbelievable, do you? Of course not. You want to be in the fullness of it. You want to be at the forefront of it. You want to be in the midst of it.

And so that is where you find yourself today. You find yourself in the midst of this or that drama, this or that activity, this or that undertaking, and it seems oh so difficult to move from here to there. And so we say now, release all of that, and know that you are Pure Essence at your core. You reside currently in this physical form for the exponential opportunity to experience what you did not understand before.

We seek to give you other tools, but you must be receptive for them. And knowing that you have not known of them perhaps in this lifetime, or maybe several others. But it is time. It is time and past time. And as you see, in another illusionary way, that sometimes there is that thing that is ready to take off, soar, and fly. But you are not there. You miss, say, the boat. Or, in this case, an airplane trip. As you go through what you have and need and find that your papers are missing. These papers are most important for they are your flight pass, your boarding pass, your ability to embark and engage in that next leg of your journey. And so what to do? What to do? *What to do …* ?

Again, we say to place that mental box upon the shelf as we seek to elaborate and extol. For you see, there is a means and methodology you might enlist. It is something you can do which is similar to perhaps what you have heard before of an on-off switch which we have just mentioned. But we would say there is more to it than that.

And so, as you look to engage what might allow for another portal of understanding, another pathway of promise to be communicated, be sure to put that mental box upon the shelf, again. We would say one more time, but we know within this life there will be many opportunities for which you will want to do the exact same thing. And that is to place that mental box upon the shelf.

It is that you have to recognize when it is time to do so. And just to allow the words to permeate and fall over your form … as rain would fall upon you, and then the water becomes absorbed by your skin. It is that absorption we seek. It is that opportunity to allow it to shower you, to transcend the mental blocking that might occur otherwise. For the mind does block what it does not accept. And so place that mental box (on the shelf) now and let us begin again.

For you see there is an on-off switch that does reside in your mental awareness, but might you allow more to be known this day? Yes, take a deep breath as you see the mental box placed upon the shelf.

Take a deep breath in. And let it out. In … and out … in … and out …

∞ *Pause to Breathe Deeply Now* ∞

Meditation

There are many portals and pathways, as we have alluded to, that are unseen. They are unseen, and so there must be that space that you prepare for them; that open space, mentally. That cavity you now see hollowed out because the box has been removed … temporarily. And you might see an on-off switch that you might now flip on. Then, keep walking in this hollowed area, and might we say also, hallowed area.

And as you move into the proximity of being from your heart center, combine the heart and the head together. See a melding of the two, almost a swirling, as there is an integration of heart and head, as you place your hands over the heart space.

Feel the integration, as you feel the heartbeat that does now proceed as we progress into this knowing. And so, you have turned on the switch. And you feel the beating of your heart. And you know all is right within the world in which you reside. All is safe in the pureness, and the holiness, and the Loving aspect which you find yourself feeling, and conveying out into the world. Stay in this space for a mere few moments, and then we will continue.

⤳ *Meditational Pause* ⤳

Tether, align, anchor with all there is. Complete a figure-eight formation which begins from the heart, and energetically encircle that which you seek. And so here we seek to know that which is beyond this life force. And we have spoken of those who are in existence in a mirrored sort of way. Those that are also a part of the Soul Essence, which is also connected and gives life to this body. And so seek to know, and hear, and understand that one that is in many ways a part of you.

And as we have discussed, may be of a higher or lower calibre. And so let us say perhaps they are of a higher calibre and you want to tether to them. But you also want to seek to communicate, discuss, and hear what they have to say at many times throughout the day. Or when you are in this posture of Loving embrace, tethering, and seeking to know more — seeking to be illumined. For as we have said, when a teacher is needed, one will appear. And is it so unusual to believe that teacher might be from within, or out, but still a part of this same Soul Essence?

And so, seek to know more. Seek to recognize more, but let us give you a pathway in which to do so. As you still the mind, focus on a figure-eight formation which connects the two together. In your mind's eye, now that you have created that space and you have the on-switch in the on position, tether now from the head to the heart with a figure-eight flow of energy.

Also, then conjecture a figure-eight flow of energy from that same heart space out into that mirrored aspect. And perhaps, the third tethering to your unseen Entourage of Light and Love so all are in accordance and rotating and vibrating together, maintaining that the mental box now is still placed upon the shelf.

And so, now, as you sit in this contemplative mode, tethering, and anchoring these things, might you then elicit questions and discernments that will formulate and flow back to you? And as we began this discussion, what about discerning between what you hear, and perhaps ego entering in, or something that is not quite of the vibration that you intend to give the answers that you seek?

As you imagine and see the energy in-flow, now let us move to the last ingredient as you enter and sprinkle Love into all that is. As you add Universal Love to the components that are in play, you see a swirling and a melding as all three figure-eight flows intertwine once more.

Now seek to hear with a discerning eye (*stet*). With a discernment that is placed upon you from the knowledge of all that is, is proceeding through Light and Love. That all that is given is given in this way. And that as you grow to do this exercise more routinely, you will hear more distinctly what is given. And it will be from a space of discernment and understanding.

You might even ask to define what you hear in a

different way other than your own voice. So what is forth-coming might be uniquely and distinctly received in a manner that is most immediately discernible from who the source is. And we ask for you to practice with this now for a mere few moments, and then we will add just a bit more to complete this thought process and this methodology.

≈ *Meditational Pause* ≈

Now that you have stored the mental loop, the mental box on the shelf, and perhaps even locked that frequency, or done some other endeavor that maximizes the ability for the mental knowingness to stay disengaged ... now, we will begin anew.

Seek to elicit a posture of Love. Seek from all that is to begin from the heart center, from the heart space, as you again engage the figure-eight flow into the mental space where the mental box did reside once before.

See this figure-eight flow as pure energy. See it rev up as a light that beams within the energy of the figure-eight flow. See the sequence and the flowing from one to the next, from that to the other as it does speed up, and the momentum does increase until it is a solid beam of light. And when this movement becomes a solid white light of energy, allow for the maximization of this charge to set in. And set the intention that now you have engaged in a new space.

And see, then, the other figure-eight formations you have created, moving in the same manner where they then seemingly become this solid white light. This light does then anchor and move down with you in an energetic way, to the center of the Earth as you release the anchoring that is there. And now you float freely from these three points of light and emerge in a brilliance of wonderment and awe.

See Universal aspects, stars, and constellations. See all that is melding and entering your line of vision. And now ask those questions which you need addressed. Ask those questions now that you are untethered, in any other way, except to these. And now seek to hear the answers, defining how you wish to hear them. If in a specific way, or tone, or something that is uniquely designed for you to know that you have aligned as you preferred. Seek this now, to play in the wonderment of all that is and to know that more can now be.

∞ *Meditational Pause* ∞

~ *Might more now be ...* ~

Chapter 6

In Readiness, All Will Grow

Do you see that often in life, you are met with adversity, which is a cloaked gift in disguise? For if you moved in the direction or continued in the pathway that you had planned, you would not be, perhaps, where you are today. Because different things became introduced, and you had to change the manner in which you were moving.

This is what we want you to focus upon today and each day moving forward. As you move and grow, you must look always, unceasingly, in a conscious sort of way, to know what other gifts and avenues are available. For if you would routinely stop, we would suggest that so would much of the adversity that comes to your door.

For when you are in a reflective state, when you are in a state of whimsical wonder, and looking at life and what you have accomplished, and what this day or that day might have been or will be, but not in a less-than energy but in a whimsical wonderment sort of way, pausing to posture how this or that might be best, you can see if you are exactly where you intended to be, or somewhere else.

So if you will do these measures, not invoking a lesser energy, not bringing forward a needy, less-than posture, then you will see that you can discover much. For it is in the posturing and the *perhaps* mode of life that you can discover what you need to discover — what Universe seeks for you to discover. What you might embrace as opposed to having some calamity befall you, some disease enter in, something other than that which you prefer because you did not stop to look otherwise.

And do you see, it is the stopping and looking and wondering that might allow for a different set of circumstances to cross your path? For now you are looking for what might be the betterment of your life. And so when you look in the wonder of all that is, when you look from the Loving posture of all that is given, then you will more easily see what is available to be seen and awaits recognition. And wouldn't that be a better way to go than to have some this or that happen within your future that is not desired?

And so, too, know that life is meant to be one of change. And when people pass from the screen of life, there is a need for almost a celebration of the life that was led. The time they were with you, the opportunities you shared, and the intrinsic things that will never pass from this screen of life or from your memory. And isn't that a better way to envision than one of loss? For don't you want what is best for the one who has made their transition? Don't you want what they want from a life that perhaps no longer offers them the value, or perhaps has already offered the value that they sought? And now it is time to move on to other objectives and other things. And so will you stop the pity party, in many ways, of those things that you have learned to embrace from a less-than level? And know that life is as it is, in a manner of speaking, because each has their own objective which you may or may not know.

For how can you know what one has set up prior to embodiment? How can you know what they knew on the inner and perhaps not in the outer? And that would suppose that you have greater knowledge, perhaps, than you do. And so release them. Release them in the joy and the wonderment of what they have discovered and are soon to discover in their next embodiment or next undertaking. Isn't that a better way to be? For life is not meant to be static, and all are not meant to stay within this life. And so many are stuck at this point. And we would say to move on, for they have moved on, and it is time for change.

Trigger, Ignite, Remember

Now we move to our next topic. And we move on to those things which we seek your attention to understand. And again, to place that mental box up upon the shelf so that it does not distract, it does not interpret, and it does not enter in where there is no use for this mental box.

We also stress within this life that you, oftentimes when trying to interpret or understand, just let the words permeate your form. Permeate your form and allow all to become intertwined and immersed in the waters that shower you with Love and information. And in many ways there is a remembering that is also triggered. In this way, you are allowing a triggering to have time to ignite. For that remembering to become unfettered; to rise up and be integrated in your general awareness once again.

And so you cannot take Heaven by storm. You cannot rush things when you are not in the position to rush them. And ego often is the culprit here that wants things quickly. Wants it right now! Doesn't want to wait! Wants to make sure that things continue to move!

But do you see that when you slow the pace, when you take a breath and breathe, that you are in a measure, and a manner of speaking, allowing? You are in a measured way of allowing more to be in your life this day. And isn't that preferred? That you recognize all that is in existence, and all that waits, and awaits your recognition?

When you consider and can see it this way, isn't that a wondrous thing? To take in life and this life, and all the beauty that does surround you when you can recognize the more that does exist and awaits your wanting to connect with it.

And so, we do greet you this day in the wonderment of all that is. In the wonderment and knowledge that life is, and offers all that you seek for it to be. And all you seek to know is available when you enlist the right tools, the right understanding in shifting your perspective to allow what you may not have considered before to be in the forefront of all that is this day.

The Importance of Your Original Purpose

When you seek to enact an objective, perhaps your life intention, your purpose, your reason for being in the nowness of this space, what thing might you do? How might you progress it, to make it manifest, sooner rather than later?

And why is there an importance here?

Why is there an importance here?

Why is there an importance here?

And we would say that it is the reason you have come into embodiment. It is the reason you have chosen to be in this Earth space. It is the reason you came and embodied to understand some thing that you did not understand when Pure Essence ... when you were Consciousness in Flow.

Do you see this thing you wanted to understand was an energy that you needed to take time to fully immerse in? So that you understood the intrinsic nature of what it is you wanted to experience and know.

And so you are here on this planet so you might understand what this energy, perhaps emotional energy, is. And to fully understand it, there must be the converse of it. And so there is that push-pull dynamic of understanding the lesser aspect before you can know the full capacity of the greater one.

This is why you came into embodiment. This is why you came into embodiment in your first incarnation. It was to know more specifically, more personally, how it felt and what it was to be in that energy. But perhaps coming into the densities of Earth, and its schoolroom, in many regards, was more difficult and more cumbersome than that one had known in spiritual form.

And so when they passed from that life into the in-between time, they found they were not able to experience that which they sought to understand. And so another life was crafted, a similar objective was put into play, known as their purpose, and they then embodied once again. But this time, there was not the fuller dynamic of that initial understanding, which was preferred. Let us say it was a minimization of what was first crafted. And this has continued over time. Each time, utilizing the life from which they evolved from to formulate and craft the next life.

And if there was a misfortune, a lesser understanding or embodiment, and perhaps even a most difficult one, when exiting that life, there would not be the full expanse of wonderment and awe to enact another life that would be better. Perhaps there was a belief that there is difficulty here on this Earth, and . . . *If I could just do thus and such, and this and that, that would be enough.* Or perhaps, *if I could enact more difficulty, then I would know more* and many other misconstrued perspectives. But never quite getting to the overarching, all-encompassing, original purpose that was postured when coming from Pure Essence, from Spirit, into physical form.

And so now, after many incarnations, there has been a degree of digressing, a degree of lessening, a degree of *not all there is* to the equation and to the components of this puzzle. And so we seek to enlighten to the fact that you did have this original mission. This original mission was what you wanted to understand, coming from Spiritual Essence into the densities of the Earth plane. And they have not been understood to the level you set out to have them be understood.

And now you are in the midst of the maya of the day.

And the maya is quite illuminating in that it illuminates so much that is in play today. You see it with illness, with plague, with death, with destruction, with all of those things that are not preferred. And they do exist in some form or fashion in every embodiment in which you have lived.

And you may take on a cause, and you may believe this cause is the most important thing that you must help to right a wrong. But do you know, and might you know, that in every lifetime there are many causes for which you can fly the flag, take up the banner, become involved? And that is not a bad thing to do. It is a good thing to move in step with righting a wrong. But we would say that, and we would hope that you would say that it is time to roll up your sleeves to get about why you are here. To get about why you have continued to incarnate on this Earth.

And it is quite simply because you have become lost in the maya that does exist here. And perhaps you believe you have discovered all you need to know because you have received inner confirmation that you have discovered all there is. And now you just need to ride out your time so you can find out that what you know is so.

You see, in this space, the illusionary is not real. And there is the belief that all that has been gleaned was exactly right and so. And then you go about planning the next incarnation and living that life. We will say that this time is not as you might believe it to be. This time is not as it appears. And you are being reinforced by what you believe to be true, as opposed to what is. For Universe seeks to make you right. Universe seeks to reinforce all you believe to be so, even when it is not. Even when what you believe to be true is the illusion you believed while embodied.

And so, ask questions in this in-between time. If you choose not to shift or change at this point, and that is fine to do, or not. But we would say to always ask questions, and to not be relegated to do this or that in an expedient way but to pause, and to question, and to ask, for we will say within this life, you cannot know all, for you are not in the space to know all because you have the mind which enters in to block and interpret.

And within each life, there is that sort of awareness that does enlist to be of assistance. But over time, it has been allowed to rule your vessel. And what we suggest here is you regain the controls. You utilize the mind and ego in their appropriateness and when it is appropriate to do so. But not to allow the controls to be taken over by that which is not consciously aware.

And so, seek this day to connect once again to your original purpose. Seek this day to know the overarching objective that your Soul had to embody on this planet long ago. Seek to know and recognize your purpose in this life is a component of that. It is a component simply because it cannot be all that it was originally because each lifetime there was not the remembering of the original one.

Recognize your original purpose is that which is the all-encompassing rationale and reason for your being here in this space. And you have gotten lost in all the objectives and causes that have turned your head and caused you to embrace that which will always need a measure of attention.

And we would say your original purpose could be a component of what you are already doing, but it is from the awareness postured when you attach to that which was the reason for your being. And when you engage from that level and from that perspective, then you look upon the occurrence differently.

So it may be this thing you are already doing but perhaps not quite the way in which you need to enlist or look upon it. But by implementing a slight shift, you might be able to do just that.

Move this day and know your original purpose is why you chose to embody in that original lifetime, having placed before you an original purpose.

But we will say the contrast (or opposing element), sometimes, have taken those who embodied out of embodiment, for they did not see the gift in the contrast that was given. The contrasting and opposing element was not seen, visibly, by the one who needed to know that countermeasure. And they did not stop perhaps and pause to ask what it might be. But then did let life direct them, Universe direct them, by introducing this countermeasure. And had they embraced the countermeasure and recognized it for what it was, they would have chuckled and been grateful. But instead chose a different path and perhaps moved out of that embodiment and into that in-between time.

And so recognize this. Recognize there is more to life. There is more to what you sought. And isn't it time to know what you wanted to know, and has moved you to reembody, and experience what you could not understand in any other way?

THE GREATER PURPOSE
Book Three: The Purpose Trilogy

Enact Your
PURPOSE

then ...
Reach for the Stars

Robyn G. Locke

GIVEN BY THE ELDERS

ENACT YOUR PURPOSE

Table of Contents

Introductory Prologue

In the beauty of the day, will you awaken to what is around you ... that which is real and that which is for your experience here? Will you look upon life with the wonderment and awe of which it is truly conspiring and inspiring within the pathway that you traverse? As All* does seek entrance into your knowingness to reach you beyond the mental aspect that does engage and enlist you to do this or that in a meaningful or not way.

And so we would say this day, might you look upon all that are the wonders of the day. All that do greet you and do express themselves to you so you see the wonderment which is all around you waiting to be exposed, as it is composed of all the things that will bring you into that space of another knowingness ... another pathway of purpose ... another aspect of being ... another way to

---

* All refers to its singular use and understanding for all are the one.

perceive and receive life so that you might not feel down-trodden and weary from your travels here.

For your journey in many ways has just begun because in this evoking of wanting, and knowing, and seeking, you then embrace all that might be in a different way. For you embrace a perspective unlike any other. You embrace that which is an expression of who you are and who you are meant to be as you traverse in this journey known as life.

And so seek this day to move in the way of wonderment for all that might be enlisted. So that each day that progresses from this one is more carefree, is more light-hearted, is more in keeping to move you to that purposeful direction which you so sought when you entered into the rounds of incarnation here.

For when you knowingly move in a manner that does progress you in a different way than perhaps before, you now see things and life within your midst differently ... do you see? You recognize the gifts given even in the negativity you once thought they evoked. You look at the colors and the fragrances, and the aspects of taste and feel and that knowing, and you recognize that it is felt differently than before. It is felt for experiential purposes and nothing more. You do not engage in the dramas of the day. You do not enlist in the dramas that present themselves, but you chuckle at their merriment and worth ... with mirth.

For you see, all elicits for you to engage from the

Conscious Awareness from that which does rest within you and does await engagement, and does seek to express itself so that you might enlist in the beauty of the day in a different way.

Enlist in the beauty of the day in a way in which you may not have engaged with that beauty and light before. Then you see life and things differently, do you see? And in that contemplative moment, in that meditative stirring of activity that is not from the mind, but from, perhaps, your heart center, that then you look upon life and do recognize that this body vessel, this Spiritual Form known as your Soul, and Source Energy have all aligned and conspired to gift you this experience.

And so we say embrace this and all life. Embrace that which is the wonderment of which it is. Embrace to know, to be in that space so that all might become known to you. So then you move in a more purposeful and aligned way — to receive and be perceived as that one of knowingness. So that then others move to emulate what you do. They do this and not that. They see the light and the mantel that you carry, for you move throughout this life in a more purposeful direction and way.

And that is what we seek throughout the gifts offered within this telling, within this book, and its pages. For as you read here, know that all is as it might be for your interpretation and the perspective that you hold. For each is that gift.

Each is that gift to be perceived and received in the time that you are accessible to its understandings and the value of what is given. For you see, if you move in the manner that you have moved in previously, you perhaps have missed some of the beauty and light which does unfold around you.

And as you recognize that these things are all gifts given so that you choose the path that is most preferred, so that you get about the business of why you incarnated here originally — why you chose that original incarnation to move into form, to feel and perceive that which was unknown from a spiritual vantage point — that which was unknown and yet wanting to be experienced and recognized … *experienced and recognized.*

Recognize and move in the manner that will gift you what you seek to experientially know and then enlist life from that vantage as you move about. Offer gratitude, and in that space of gratitude, do elicit those things that you have recently discovered. Elicit those things so that then they go out to Universe, are multiplied, and returned back to you as you know.

For many times it is not the knowing, but it is the doing that is amiss and missing from the landscape of your life … for you have gathered much knowledge. You have gathered and tucked it away ever so safely so it is accessible when you are ready to engage and move in that manner.

But we say, do not put off what you might do today. For

there is opportunity in this and each day moving forward as you progress in this life. There is opportunity. And there is that which is what we would say wonderment and allowing, as there is that entrance into this world of form.

And so see life as fluid and flowing. See life as ever-changing ... expanding, and contracting based upon your actions and efforts — based upon what you seek to know — based upon what you seek to find — based upon what you look to engage with ... this day.

Enlist this day with Love. Begin this day in Love and call Universal Love into the platform of your daily awareness. Express It. Move It out into the world of form. Express this Love and the wonderment that It is. And in so doing, more will return back to you. More will be in that space for you to be in the space of Loving embrace. And then your days will be fuller, and you will move back into the world of form that which is a necessary and needed component.

For you see, all life is healed and made whole through the energy of Universal Love and Its engagement in this day.

I received the Introductory Prologue and the first five chapters of this book, Enact Your Purpose, *in Lesvos, Greece. Might you be receptive to receiving this gift of Love? Undertake to embrace their measures, words, and these pages so all might evoke a remembering as you step through the veil to know more of what is yet to be.*

How to Receive to Perceive

Do you see that all is possible when you begin from the heart space? Begin in that way each time you read here. Ask for clarity and understanding. Set the intention that more is to be. Set the intention to read with your heart as opposed to your head. Seek and ye shall find. Move in an unbridled way. Each time you stop or pause reading, begin again by focusing on your heart and asking for more to be. Ask for more to be understood, and that you move always in the clarity of Love.

Given by the Elders

Chapter 1

Awaiting Focus

As we consider the best starting point for these discussions and all that is to move forward, we ask you to center your focus and to be in that space of Loving embrace. That you might know, and be inclined to know, something that has been lost perhaps in time but is still accessible through these messages, recordings, insightful gifts.

And so, do embrace each thing moving forward. Embrace each as you move to adopt and adapt to insights gleaned as you seek more. Might we move this day to be in that oneness, so that you might express and illuminate those offerings in a most expedient and Loving way?

Might You Sharpen Your Focus Now

Might you consider moving in the manner that does not restrict the flow and all that might be imparted this day?

We seek to give you Loving insights and those things which will propel your steps forward in a most expedient way.

You see, we center and focus upon that which you seek and which you sought before coming into human form. But because of the densities that are in play and in place, and all that exists within the physicality of this life experience, do you see that many components that were unseen were lost over time and over the many incarnations that perhaps the one or the other has experienced? And so know that although time does not exist here as it does there, that there is a need in this time, to consider moving and stepping up what has existed before so that you do not continue in the rounds of incarnation on this Earth platform.

And so we have come, and there are many who have traveled and tarried here so that this objective might be realized ... for there are those who have been lost here for a time and believe that the dramas within the day are those things which are necessary for them to engage in. And by this, we mean that those who had once sought or wanted to achieve certain objectives and understandings that they then have the opportunity to return to why they embodied in the first place.

But when various activities or undertakings are seen as a need to correct, a need to engage with to perhaps change the flow in which they currently exist, so that truth does prevail. So that honor does prevail. So that justice does prevail. Then they turn away from that which they might ordinarily seek to know, to right that wrong.

And we will tell you that within each lifetime, there have been those things which have drawn one or the other into an activity that is all-consuming. And the rightness of a wrong is a just thing. And bringing justice to an unjust situation is a good thing. And so we do not say that one supersedes the other, but rather, might you consider that now is the time to move about this life so that you might enact why you came here and what you set up into motion in doing so.

We will share, as discussed in *The Original Purpose* book, that when you moved into that in-between state, oftentimes, although you believed you know all, that this is not so. That at this point, you know as you knew on Earth when you were physically placed. And so, although you may believe you are right, and just, and deser*ved* of the understanding you now hold, and the belief you hold — that those may be as they were gleaned on this Earth platform.

In other words, you carry with you that understanding. You carry with you the understandings that you held while physically placed. And so, although you are given reinforcement, you then do not move from a more enlightened space. And it is then that you carve out your next life experience, and it is using faulty material. It is using not complete information. It is done using that information which you currently believed while in embodiment.

So there is not the stepping up perhaps, although this is not always the case. But there is often not the full totality of understanding that would allow that next embodiment to be more enlightened and moving forward from a more aligned space.

This is the methodology, and the purpose of these books. It is to give you more for consideration and contemplation. And as always, we advise that you seek a centeredness and a moving within to determine if these teachings are right for you. And if they will expand what you currently know as these understandings cause what you understand to grow.

And so this day, as we begin this next chapter of your life, as you weave it into the considerations that exist within your being and world, might you know that all moves in this way in Love, for we are the energy of Love. And we seek for you to anchor and be in the space where Loving embrace can be accepted, acknowledged, and incorporated into your day moving forward in a most Loving way.

For all does move as the ebb and flow of the ocean or the seas that surround, for there is a Loving, wafting energy that does become immersed and incorporated within the dynamic of the one who does seek engagement there.

So know that this Earth does offer many beautiful and wondrous opportunities to still the mind. To still the racing contemplations that the mind actually throws into the path of the one who is, what we would call, a seeker.

Know that the many checklists, the many objectives that the mind and especially egoic mind do produce within one's day ... that they are all not necessary. And that in the doings that are suggested and proposed, as you move about, are actually distractions that keep you from moving in a most and more expedient way to the path of your enlightenment.

You see, you came to understand an energy. You came to understand an energy that we will call your purpose or mission for being in this life. And that purpose or mission is unique unto you. You set out a platform; you set out an objective; you set out something that you wished to undertake and know more fully. And in doing so, you must also experience its converse energy. For it is in the converse, or the opposite (opposing) energy, that you discover the full totality of that which you wish to know.

Many individuals that chose to embody in the delicate nature of their Soul Essence, and not having experienced the densities of the Earth platform in previous times, did quite literally get taken out of embodiment when their converse energy, or that opposing energy, introduced itself into their life path. For it was a shock, oftentimes, to experience that which was not in alignment with what was sought.

Without having a clear understanding of what they were stepping into, the Soul Essence, in its naivety of what was to befall them, did not know how to react or how to take in what was being given. And perhaps, let us say, they did not perceive or receive what was given as a gift. They do not look upon it in the whimsical wonderment that it was.

And so often in this way, many lifestreams did pass from the physical platform into that in-between time. And it is there that the strategizing, and the planning, and putting forth of the next life path does take place. But you see within the undertakings of the original purpose in that original lifetime, there is not the full awareness, moving forward, of that which they knew before because the understanding of where they came from, and what their objective was, was now a bit masked.

And they did not remember what they had set out and put into play. And they did not remember their divine heritage. They remembered components of the life from which they had just passed. And we will say too that beliefs are carried with the one, into this next phase. And so, although there is not the full recall, there is the general understanding of what might be and what is wanted. But it is from a more fragmented formation. In other words, there is not the totality of understanding or recall.

There are components that are recalled, and there are

delineations of what was in occurrence in that lifetime. But it is almost, we would say, the big picture of the life experience that is photographically recalled and given (but) in a most Loving way, but without the mind or ego inserting during this time.

But you see, the structuring and the moving from the lifestream, from physicality to this in-between time and then back into embodiment, does not have all of the parameters and all the components that it once knew before physically embodying the first time. In other words, there is not the totality of understanding that was given and held by the Soul Essence upon that initial embodiment.

And so as embodiments occur successively, there is less and less of a recall of the objective that was sought. And so now you have many lifestreams that have been incarnating for many, many, many rounds of embodiment. And we would say there are those who believe that this is all there is. And we will say this is as it is for a purpose, but it has lost some of the core and intrinsic components that would allow the one to reconnect to their original mission and their original purpose for incarnation.

And we have sought and do now seek for that recon-nection to be further anchored and recognized. And so we have given books, and blog posts, and teachings that will allow the one to have the opportunity for that insight to bubble up to the surface … to bubble up and to be known. For oftentimes, the mind does confound for it cannot understand much beyond its own measure. And so these more lofty undertakings are not within its realm of consideration.

And so perhaps your mind does wander — perhaps your mind does fixate and focus upon one thing and not another. And so you miss valid considerations that are no longer a part of the dynamic because you quite frankly do not hear them. Or you resonate with something that does sound familiar, but you miss the newer components that are given that might help you strategize as you move about this life to choose and make better choices. Or those choices which will move you in the direction preferred. For we will say that there is no good or bad choice, for each will move you in the direction which you seek for that expansiveness and that directive to be embraced.

So now let us say that as you seek to know, and as you seek to align into the oneness of All that is, might you do so from the posture of Love and Loving embrace? Of knowing that these things are given so that you might better navigate this life moving forward ... so that you might better navigate all you seek to know. So that at the conclusion of this life, you might no longer incarnate into this Earth platform but move in a manner free from the constrictions and the requirements of embodiment.

There is the need prior to departing here to bring

wholeness and completion to the Soul Essence, which may have been coming here for quite a time. For you see, there are those different things that do occur that splinter a Soul. And so always seek to move, and to regroup, and regain, that which was lost in time and over time.

When regaining and joining together those components that were fractured or splintered away from the Spiritual Essence, then there is the totality of the Whole that does then have the opportunity to reclaim all components of Itself or of Its Being.

And so always seek wholeness in each regard … wholeness to bring that clarity so that there is not that fractured state when moving from this (physical) plane to another.

◇ *Enlist The Following Instruction*
Contemplatively or Meditatively ◇

And so now we seek that centeredness. And we ask for you to place (your) feet firmly upon the floor with your hands in a manner that will allow for energy to effortlessly and effectively move throughout your being and form. We ask for you to see light swirling about as it comes from all directions above you, entering into the vessel that you know as your personality or self.

See it fully embrace each cell, organ, and body part so that there is a Light Energy that does infuse and flow throughout you. Now see that light traveling from your form, down through your feet, and down into the center of the Earth.

Now see a swirling, and an anchoring, and a Loving embrace that comes from the energetic flow of that substrata of Earth as it moves to embrace you. Then, feel each moving out to fully encircle and anchor you into the form in which you now reside.

The energy then travels back from that anchoring position and posture into the body form, giving you the anchoring of this Earth platform as you move about the day, so you do not flit and float throughout the process of your undertakings.

See Light Energy infuse and engulf you now. See Light Energy sparkle and be that effervescent light that does permeate and saturate your form. Feel a renewal as Love anchors you into the physicality of your existence now. And know that Loving support and guidance is with you always.

Call to those who reinforce your lifestream in prayer, in meditation, in contemplation, and in all activities as you seek to know more — for there are those who travel with you concurrent to each embodiment that are there to answer your calls and questions. They have an energetic connection to you. And in that energetic connection, you can hear, and see, and know their responses. Perhaps not to physically see them but to see signs that you determine and establish along the way.

And so as these signs, and platforms, and understandings are embraced, and you do recognize them as being gifts to know which way to go when you do move in a more enlightened and, might we say, inspired way. Always seeking and asking to know that path which will propel you in the right direction for you to accomplish all you seek to know.

For you see, this is the yearning. This is the wanting. This is the determination that you have sought, and that is perhaps amiss in this lifetime now. For when there is a lack of fulfillment — when there is a hole, let us say, within your world that does not seem to be filled and infused, as it might be, it is because there is a lacking of that which is sought and was sought in another time once, perhaps, long ago.

And so, do not tarry. Do not focus upon that which is not in alignment, but focus on those things which will propel your steps forward. Seek insights through meditational ways. Seek that knowingness from within as you engage first, always through the heart center as opposed through mental ponderings. For the mental-ness will not get you there. It will reinforce that which is not. It will reinforce that which is more, perhaps, egoic, but we would say that it will not lead you to where you truly seek to go. For you see, all of the wonderment is there waiting for you to embrace it — waiting for you to recognize it — waiting for you to incorporate it into your being and world as you move in this manner moving forward.

As we proceed, we ask for you to move in that alignment of the oneness of all that is. To move into the alignment of all that might be. To move into the alignment that will help you navigate this life in a way in which you have not navigated before. All life seeks to embrace you in the Loving expanse it does offer. And it is only the awareness, and the wanting, and the looking, and the desiring of that which is to be — that all might be more readily attained.

And so this is what we seek this day: that you will look at life in the wonderment that it is. That you will not be caught and trapped within the dramas of the day. That you will move beyond what appears to be taken from you in the injustice that does seemingly exist.

And recognize that there must be a right and wrong in order to see the good and the bad, in order to see the wanted and the unwanted, so that there is a feeling component that you can align with and know that this is preferred and this is not. For if only light were shown, there would not be the diversity or the differing mannerisms of that which was sought in a way that was not known before.

For you see, if you knew these things, you would not be here. If you knew these things, you would not have taken embodiment. And so recognize that the converse was necessary so that you might have the full expanse of the totality of that which you sought to know. And so that is the purpose of the diversity, and perhaps perceived negatively, that does exist, but when you do so — when you view each, when you engage with the knowledge that this is a part of the plan, then you can look upon it differently. And you do not feel that you have been imposed upon or infringed upon, but now you look upon it as an opportunity for expansion.

And that is what we seek to impart here. That is what we seek for you to know. That is what we seek for you to do and embrace in a more conscious way so that all the dots are connected … so that in this lifetime, you do so in the consciousness and the Loving embrace in which many of these activities exist. For we would say those activities that you believe to be of a negative nature are, as we have said before, gifts. Gifts to be recognized, unwrapped, and seen for what they truly are.

And when you move in this manner, when you move in this awareness, when you move in this way, life appears differently. And now you look at life in the conscious awareness in which you now exist, and it becomes surreal. It no longer feels heavy, weighted, and in the density in which it is. For that is the Earth experience. For without the full feeling component, there is not the potentiality of the possibility for more to be known in this way.

And so move this day in this way, and see how your day does unfold. See how your day does unfold, and how the beauty of the day then can progress, and be all that it might be, had aligned to be, in this wanting as it wafts and floats about. Anchor now and know moving forward that more is to be given.

Chapter 2

Moving into Alignment

As we proceed, further anchor in Light and Love moving forward in the wonderment of what might be. We will say there is much which is known, but much more which remains unknown, and that which is on the precipice of entry back into this world of form. For it has been remiss or missing from being recognized in this time and space.

And so as you anchor into these words and into all that is, know that it is in many regards a remembrance of what was once known and understood intrinsically. And so allow yourself to read and hear these words, and for a bubbling up to occur within your system. For it is in many ways the allowing of what was once known and understood to be recalled, remembered, and once again gleaned as a part of the understanding from which you operate.

There is this component, known as the body vessel. And the body vessel anchors and harbors much. And as we have touched upon and talked about in the *Awaken* book, there is much that occurs within the day and within the facilitation of the body that occurs without thought or interjection by you, conscious awareness.

As you consider and muse upon this now, might you recognize that it is a rather large undertaking — that you ingest food, digest food, shift, adjust within the day to activities and undertakings that cause your body to need to effortlessly shift from one mode into the next. And we would like for you to consider that now for just a moment as you conceptualize all that your body does undertake and move to embrace within the day. Might you do so now?

∽ *Conceptualization Pause* ∽

As you reflect here once again, might you see that it is a rather large undertaking and that were you to need to incorporate instruction and direction, as far as perhaps your heartbeat and the regulation of your blood flow, that this would be an ongoing process? For you see, each must occur ongoing and effortlessly throughout your day. And so were that to be the objective, and the premise, and the purpose for your activities within the day, you would be engaged as such in a mental mind bog to have this or that activity occur.

And so consider further, as you move about and

perhaps you take a tumble or run a race, and now you are out of breath, or have another occurrence within your system that you must stop and regulate, how this would further layer upon that which is.

And then to take it even a step further as you consider the emotional energy that becomes anchored and stored within your body ... that this energy is gathered and accumulated within this form. And it does then shift and change all that was there before. And as this becomes recognized, and as this becomes quantified, you then must address this or that energetically. And you do see that all of this would take time in order for you to process and to adequately maintain.

As you muse and consider this further, we ask for you to recognize that your body, its importance, and the vessel from which you know as your being or your personality, is intertwined with that Spiritual Essence which did then enter in, and commingle one with the other, so that you are able to experience life in the densities in which life does exist here.

It is as if you were putting on a spacesuit to go out and do a spacewalk that you need certain components in which to breathe. You need certain components in which to move and navigate about. You need certain components in which you might exist in the reality in which you find yourself.

There is the one, the vessel — the body form — and

there is the other, the Pure Conscious Awareness. And the two were needing to merge and meld together so that there might be the full totality of experience in a more seamless and effortless way. And so you see, there are those writings which have discussed the vessel in a more complete form. And so you might research that if you prefer more than what we will give and provide here.

There is the body vessel. Within the body vessel, there are certain characteristics and properties that are maintained mentally. And the mental aspect, which we have stressed before and others have done so as well, that is not a part of the Conscious Awareness from which you reside … there is that incessant and compelling dialog that does routinely occur.

It is advisable to always respond to the mental understandings and underpinnings in a way of reflection, but not in a way of ownership. For these do continue on incessantly. In recent times, there has been more of an understanding that this mental prodding is a part of that which is considered self. And we now want you to consider that this is *not* a part of you. It is separate and aside from you and it is nothing that need be maintained, judged, or engaged with in any way other than the recognition that it does exist.

We further want to recommend that when these mental opinings occur, that you reflect upon them and consider briefly if it is something moving from a more conscious awareness standpoint, or that small voice that also operates within, or if it is more of a demanding egoic measure that you need to place aside, chuckle at, and continue on ... for we will also say that the mind is *not* you.

The mind is and does relegate the activities of the body, and that body vessel does need maintenance 24/7. And do you see, because the maintenance occurs from morning until night and then in between while you sleep, that this mental voice also operates within that same time parameter? But it is meant to be something that you use as a tool. But not knowing that it is a tool, the tool has taken over the assembly line.

And so we would say also that as you consider this and that, that you recognize that it is like the computer taking over at the location where the mainframe is in play. And in that consideration, that the computer is now running that which the operator should be running. And the operator is standing by as the computer does orchestrate what plays and occurs and what programs are run while the operator sits and listens patiently to what the computer might advise.

We would encourage then for that to be shifted. And for you to recognize that this is not the design that was originally set up within the formatting and planning of this enterprise and in this collaboration ... for there is, in many ways, a collaboration of what is occurring.

There is the body vessel, and there is the Spiritual

Consciousness. And the two were needed, are needed, in order for the operation to seamlessly and effectively occur within the existence here. And do you recognize that over time the awareness has been lost of the intricacies and the connection between the two?

And so we do want you to know that the awareness might be recognized once again. For you are not the body vessel, you are not the mind. You are not those things which appear to be you because within the densities that exist here, you needed that spacesuit in order to breathe, in order to navigate, in order to exist in the time and space in which you now reside. And so, not knowing these things, not recalling, and existing through multiple incarnations having let go of that which you cannot see, we want you to recognize this once again. For it will help with the understanding, and the compartmentalizing, and the releasing of the mental egoic voice that is so incessantly playing within the background of your day.

As you consider life, and as you consider different opportunities, and certain things are interjected, or incessantly pronounced within the playings and the activities that the mind does profess, we want you to recognize that it is not real, that it is unnecessary, and that you chart your own course. But you must be aware that the mind is not you. So that when it recommends this or that, when it suggests different activities that take you off-course or in a different direction than you might otherwise be, we want you to be the conscious awareness. We want you to be consciously aware of what it is doing. And in that conscious awareness, you can then consider life and the things that are suggested mentally in a different way.

For it is in the understanding, and the perceptions held that you then can make different choices within life because now you no longer see life through the limited mental scope in which you may have seen life before. For how were you to know that the mental promptings that you have been receiving are not your own? And we would say to consider the body vessel as a large computer with various programs and various considerations that must be prompted, refueled, energized, and kept in play.

Yet you, as conscious awareness, are a being that needs to be refueled, but it is through the stilling of the mind. It is through the separation from the mind. It is from the resetting and restoring of that which was understood much more easily before.

So now consider the body vessel and consider the Soul Awareness. And that they do meld and merge together in the oneness in which they now reside within this Earth plane, and within the dynamic of the day and within the doings of the day. And how they do ceaselessly communicate and work together. Yet, there are those components that take the body vessel down a path that would make it harder for it to operate and be in the polarity and the oneness of all that it might be and all that it is.

And so those choices made throughout the day of what to eat, what to drink, what to ingest, what to participate in, what to play in, what to activate or not within the system are those components which either elevate and fortify or diminish and retard. And so throughout the day, it is greatly recommended that you stay consciously aware of all that you are fueling within the choices, and the opportunities, and the components that are enlisted from those things that are selected for you to participate in, ingest and enjoy.

We do not suggest that you live a puritanical life or that you limit all types of foods at all times. But we would say that limiting what you ingest and doing so in a more conscious way is the solution, in many cases, to negative issues that seem to arise when there is no curfew given to the teenager who engages in activities they know are not advised.

As you consider foods and different varieties of those things that you choose to ingest, know that all will fuel your body accordingly. And so, you will want to research those food groupings that will facilitate the best flow for your form. Know that as you incorporate these new considerations, or existing ones into your daily dealings, that it will infuse your body in a way perhaps that it has not been fueled before. For you see when you do things from a conscious awareness standpoint, and you move into the flow of the day, incorporating beneficial components into your choices and into your selections, your body has the benefit of these choices and selections.

You need not be concerned and overly cautious as you move about to experiment with this or that but rather to see how your body responds when you shift and change what goes into its form. Digestion and other considerations will more easily occur when different food groupings are chosen or time is considered as to when, and how often, and how much to eat. You see, these are all components that help to fuel the body in a more appropriate way.

As you move about within this day and you choose those different food groupings that benefit the objective from which you move now amongst the day, might you say it is to maintain a healthy vessel, a healthy body, and one that will propel you forward in the later years of your life?

For if you move as earlier in life, with no consideration for your later years, you may burn the candle at both ends and find that when you move about to focus on a more purpose-driven outcome, that there is not the body capacity to fulfill what you wish to accomplish.

And so this is the rationale and the preference of protecting and supporting the body; it is that you work in coalition and in collaboration with this vessel form. And that you recognize that it is temporary. It is something that is not carried with you from this life to the next. And so it is a temporary container that does house many things for your use throughout this lifetime. But if you do not recognize and see it as a temporary form, then you may not take the proper care and maintain the best oversight of this vessel.

So what might you do as you consider food choices? And as you are about and in the day, how will you enlist better choices? For the mind does prompt you to try this and try that and *mmmm* how good this would taste and how another would be so worthwhile and perhaps make life more fun. And especially when considering drugs and other stimulants of a nature that are not of benefit, how do you enlist oversight so that the choices are those that are preferred and will allow for the maximum usage of this body vessel?

For you see, you find yourself in a collaboration. You find yourself in the mix of wanting to know how this or that might feel — yet not perhaps knowing the full outcome of the choices in the time in which you make the determination. And what about considerations of addiction, of those things ingested? Might you now move to recognize that those too must be a consideration of the choices that you then enlist or not into the daily dealings of what, we will say, is life here?

And so enjoy those things that you see, and you would

like to try, but do so in small measure. And when you recognize if they impose an ill effect upon you mentally, which is to say on your body, then you might move away from larger quantities that might take you down a path that would be harder to reverse or not embark upon in a bigger way the next day.

In other words, sometimes cravings magnify and grow and become that which is unsustainable for the body to perform its daily dealings and duties to maintain life here as you know it and enjoy it. And so be the good steward of your body vessel and form so it might anchor you into the objectives, into the accomplishments you set out to understand and know once, perhaps long ago.

And now we shift slightly to another topic within the same parameter, but we ask for you to consider this in a more whimsical way so your mind might get around something it may not otherwise understand. We ask you to consider now a third dynamic within the mix of these dealings. We ask for you to consider not only the body vessel and the Conscious Awareness that do navigate to intertwine together, but a third component not often discussed or understood. Consider now a third ingredient into the mix of the dynamics of this body, or might we say personality — for the personality does incorporate many things. It does incorporate the vessel, the Conscious Awareness, and that unknown third ingredient that oversees the mix and is the glue that holds it all together.

We would say to move into that alignment so that you might be receptive to receive. Move into the alignment and the knowingness that so much is unknown, that much has been lost in time, and that we are in the time and space to bridge that awareness of what is yet to be because it already is, do you see? Do you see that there is that which is in existence, but perhaps unknown to the mental knowingness — that we would say is the mental egoic knowingness of what is understood within the day?

Now we shift into that discussion so that you might have a greater awareness of what this body does truly harbor in addition to those known ingredients. We move to discuss the third, the Intrinsic Knowingness, and the Overseer of all. That component is the source and the energy from which you are derived. And it is Source Energy that collaborates amongst the two to bring them into the fruition you see within the personality that does aspire to achieve in this platform.

Source Energy — God Source — is the glue that brings the two together and keeps this body, what we might say, functioning, and operating, and alive. For without the three components working in unison and in union together, there would not be the functioning of the body with the consciousness as Source Energy is the glue.

Chapter 3

Shifting Sands of Time

Within life and the complexities found within the day-to-day dealings with life in general, you will find that much is not as it is presumed to be. And in fact, much of what the mind presumes is factually incorrect. And so, as you enlist to learn and discover more, you will have, let us say, a degree of backlash from the mind, in that the mind does seek to control and navigate the vessel which it has now commandeered. It does seek to circumvent, to a degree, you attaining that knowledge, for it is in many ways the diminishment then of the mind and mind's control over the vessel.

And do you see at many levels, there is a control issue at play within life in general by those who orchestrate grander objectives for those who are inhabitants here, but then again also mentally by the mind which does navigate the vessel in how it does proceed and what it does perceive.

If you enlist from the wonderment of a child those steps that will enable you to look upon the vessel and the activities that surround the vessel, then you remain consciously aware and in more of a questioning mode. Not in a needy way of asking because you do not know and are fearful, but in a wonderment sort of way. In the general parameters of the loveliness and the potentialities that might otherwise be in existence were you to allow them to be.

For do you see that the mind is a dicey deal? The mind seeks to circumnavigate and circumvent the awareness from regaining enough awareness to seek a recapturing or a reckoning of losing its grasp and grip over the vessel which it now has commandeered and controls.

And so you must want this much more than you do perhaps at this point in time. For if you had wanted it previously, you would perhaps not be in the mind game in which you find yourself. And so we seek now to start with this rather than that. So that as you set about to listen, read, or understand what is being given, you do so with more clarity because you understand the constraints with which these words might be received if you do not recognize that there will be opposition to the understanding of them.

And so you may choose to put this book down. You may choose to not listen any longer. You may choose to place this book back upon the shelf to inquire and learn more another day. And this is where we would say that you must push through a degree of this — push through what is now rising to the surface. Push through the inclination to no longer listen or intently digest these words.

For you see, the mind is a dicey deal, and it does seek … control. And it does seek to take control, maintain control, and be in control of all that moves forward within your life. For that is its program; that is its intent. That is its relentless and unpausing nature.

You as conscious awareness must, at this point, navigate appropriately so that it does recognize that there is another captain that has now joined the ship. And that captain seeks to run things a little bit differently. And so do seek to know that the captain is in control and does so with Loving measure. Does so in reverence of what is in the midst of all who recognize what is in play and underway.

We seek for you to know that with the three components that join together to bring life into this body and allow your Spiritual Consciousness to navigate in this terrain, we let you know that there is a purpose that was devised once long ago. And that purpose would allow that Spiritual Consciousness to enact and know an energy that It did not quite understand in a physical way. It did not quite understand how this or that energy would feel were It to step into a position of knowing. And so, It sought to expand and know more.

There was an agreement that was entered into by the

Soul, as there are certain parameters by which the Soul must agree … before entering into this Earth platform. So it is not an accident. It is not as a result of a misunderstanding. There is a clear path and a clear understanding of what was wanted — is wanted and is now in play. And we seek for you to remember components of this. Perhaps not mentally for that has been blocked, but to have a sense or feeling that this is so.

And so, we seek this day for you to engage in such a way that you enter into a contemplative mode to feel the words that are evoked rather than to mentally try to decipher what is being given. This, to some degree, is resisted. And so, it is truly the incorporating of the words at a more intrinsic level that will get you to where you seek to go.

Recognize there was an agreement. And in this agreement, you would garner certain things similar to donning a spacesuit, as we interjected previously. And by donning this spacesuit, you could breathe within the environment, you could blend in with other inhabitants who operated there and who operate there, and you could accomplish what you seek and sought to understand.

In addition, you are given and have with you an unseen entourage which we have referred to in previous times. And there is no set number within your entourage, but they are not seen, oftentimes not known, and they do enter into the stage of your life when you invite them in.

And that invitation comes in the form of prayer, asking insightful questions, meditative or contemplative questions, questions before you go to sleep at night, or those ponderings that you engage with throughout the day. For now you are in seeking mode, and they await that opportunity because at that time you are receptive to receive.

And so, we have referred to them as the great mimickers. We have referred to them as the ones that do step in to enlist answers when perhaps you've called to another. For it is their opportunity, you see, to delve into assisting what they know you have intrinsically requested. And that is why you hear and have known that God Source, or such a source as Source Energy, or some other title used to represent Omnipotence and that OmniPresent Power that is about you and about this space all of the time.

For you are, they are, and All that is does operate with that Spark of Divinity. And so, it is simply that you have donned a robe of mortal-dom while on this planet. So that you could experience what you did not understand previously, and this is why you are here. This is why you chose to come into physical form. So that you could know the extremes of that which you sought to know, so that you knew more of the depth of which that thing is.

We will say that the thing that is the creative production of the energy you sought to create is the byproduct of what it is you want to understand. And so don't you see that you can be doing it in any number of ways? It is the energy that you keep in the doing. And so if the thing that you once loved no longer feels as it once did and now feels sticky, dense, weighted, heavy, unwanted, then you must release that and move on to this other thing. This thing that makes your heart sing. This thing that makes you feel that all is possible and makes you look forward to the next day, and gives you that bounce within your step ... don't you see?

And so, it is all about the feeling component. And when the feeling component shifts, you must shift-change too. You must shift-change so that you can mirror this rather than that as you move your alignment to be in oneness with something that is preferred.

We would say there is a degree of inwardly knowing this. But sometimes you are in the midst of one activity or another, or living in one spot rather than another, or in existence in a way that turns into something that is not preferred, and you resist the change that is required for you to move back into that Loving embrace, that Loving space, that space that you might enlist that would give you that more preferred feeling energy.

This is the present moment awareness that is so critical or is so important for you to understand and maintain. For if you are mentally engaged and are in a mind activity most of the time, you do not acknowledge that these things do not feel as they might or as they should. And we seek for you to regain a measure of that once again. We seek for you to regain the proximity of Love and Loving embrace that you must maintain, to a degree, so that you can navigate this life more appropriately, and make better choices, and see better options, and enlist better perspectives. So that your perspectives are those which make you feel better to be in the space in which you reside.

And that is what we seek to impart here. For the agreement is simply with this unseen entourage that they navigate you in a more appropriate way that keeps you, in many regards, directed to the right choices that will move you and keep you in alignment with the Agreement that was established so long ago.

The Agreement keeps you on the path toward your original purpose. The difficulty yet is that in this day, most know about the life purpose but very few recall or engage with their original purpose. And we have explained it in a number of ways, but let us say in the newness of this space that there are life purposes that are given within each embodiment, and they have a component or a degree of understanding that are a component of the original purpose. But until the original purpose is enacted, there is the returning to complete what was begun once, perhaps long ago.

And so there is no timetable for completion, for you see you did come from a space of no time. And time here is another illusionary component, for there is simply energy and a boundless opportunity to engage — to learn what is wanted.

When Soul Essence entered into form, there was not the concern that this or that would take a long time to gather or ascertain. And in fact, many thought that the original embodiment would facilitate all they sought to know. The difficulty here was that the densities that they entered into were greater than they perhaps understood previously. And they did not anticipate how things would feel. And they did not anticipate what the mind would impose within the space of not knowing. For it was not an elevated instruction that was given. It was more of a fight or flight or rudimentary sort of instruction that was imposed upon this delicate life force.

And so that, coupled with ego, entered in to give something other than the pure Love and direction that might otherwise have been proffered. And so many times the life force in that original incarnation did pass either abruptly or from a lackluster response to the various energetic components that were in play. And by this we mean, oftentimes, there was so much coming at the one that they did not move as they might have believed while spiritually placed, for the densities felt here are felt in a different way and are much more significant than perhaps previously believed.

Know this day, that as you listen, as you read, as you

understand this from the platform from which you now reside, that you have been incarnating perhaps for quite a time. And so we seek that you marinate with this, and you then be the marinade within it so that you understand what is being given.

Might you pause now in meditative contemplation, focusing first on your heart space and recognizing that questions posed might begin from that space as opposed to mentally? For the mental space will leave you adrift and give you confirmations that are not preferred, for they will move you more in a mental premise than in a heart space premise. And will give you answers that will require additional insights and direction later, for they do not take you on the direct route you seek.

Seek now to know from that Loving embrace, from that Loving space that you have carried within and is still accessible even in this day. For it is always with you, it is always about you, and it is always ready to place you in the best footing for what might now be as you move beyond this space and into that Loving embrace.

As you enlist a meditational pause, might you listen to uplifting music and then ask to know more? Have a journal or laptop near you. And so as you ask the question —*Might I know more?* – allow the answer that appears to come into your awareness, and then write it down. Write down anything else that comes in during this time. We would say that although the music may not be engaged here, you might play musical engagements on your own as you focus upon the question:

Why am I here, and what now might I know to engage this process in a manner that will allow me to know more ... allow me to move in unrestricted ways to engage what I once sought to understand more deeply?

Pose questions, elicit answers, and know the answers are coming forth because you have willed them out of their dormant space, their private space, their proximity into the nowness of this time.

∾ *Meditational Pause* ∾

We seek for you to know that there is more than what you may physically or mentally perceive. And so we move forward to provide additional components that are necessary for you to have the full encapsulation, the full personification, the full understanding of what this body, this life, this experience, and how it has been assembled, how it has been extrapolated, how it has occurred. We seek for this to be known by you once again.

And so, do you see that all life is a mystery in many ways? For there are many presumptions and assumptions as to how you got here and why you are here. And also how your body is and how it came to be.

We will say it is not of that lowly design that is promoted oftentimes, but it is a higher design and a design that was brought about so that you might experience life in the full totality that it might be — in the lightness of being of which it is. But sometimes, there are choices made that facilitate changes within the body — that spark and ignite different potentialities to be in cue and in existence. And so, these do alter what was perhaps planned upon or established formerly.

Know that as you navigate and move about here, and as you circumnavigate sometimes the globe of this world, there are things that you experience and see, and there are other components that exist within the mix of your day and in the background of activities and of surroundings that are not apparent or as perceived.

There are many levels to this life which you live. You perhaps travel and go somewhere where there is a familiarity and a comfort level in reaching that location. Yet this location was formerly unknown. And we have discussed this in the *Awaken* book, but we would say that there are deeper components to those pathways you travel and experiences that perhaps were sought formerly or in another period in time, and there is an energy that perhaps still emanates there that does ebb and flow within the mix of the day and within all that does exist, having reconnected to that energy once again.

Know that as you ponder these things, that life will continue to be that mystery. That wonderful enterprise that is not fully known or conceptualized by the mind and the limitations imposed by the mind, for it cannot conceptualize many things beyond its immediate parameter of understanding.

As you move about in this life, and you seek to incorporate new understandings, the mind sometimes rejects or does not hear what is brought forward. And so we would say to allow sometimes the words and the insights to permeate and to saturate and then to allow the bubbling up of the intrinsic understanding that does result. It is the deeper, more recognized, more wanted feeling component that does then emanate from there.

Life is and does equate the result of anticipation sought. The result of anticipation sought and what is to then be gleaned. For each is that which it is and awaits entry into your understanding and into this world of form.

So as you think about the body mechanics and the body vessel per se, and you recognize that it has many duties that you may not be fully aware of, having perhaps covered them in school or not, or having recognized that it is a complex organism that does require oversight and guidance, good fueling, good tooling, good mechanisms that keep it operational and functional throughout the duration of the mechanism or organism that is now in consideration and play.

We will say that when you leave this life, and there is no longer the need for the vessel, the vessel then does decay, for it is no more — for the activation component was the Soul Essence. The Soul Essence commingled with the Source Energy. It did provide life and the merging and melding together of the three-in-one.

As you consider this further, recognize that a Soul is needed to encapsulate that which did not need encapsulation before ... for Spirit Essence is unbounded and is unlike as perhaps perceived, but when it moves into the body form, it does need that Soul encapsulation. And so, there is a minimization in the process from the expansive energy, into Soul, into body.

As you muse upon this now, consider the vastness of being which your being has been and will soon again be. For life does have an ebb and flow, and there is much, much more to life in general than simply this life. For you did come from a vastness of understanding, and in that totality of being, you did want to seek more. You did want to understand and know what something felt like. You wanted to know what something felt like and how it would be to experience this or that emotional energy ... this or that emotional energy, this or that experience, this or that activity, this or that creation.

And so, you did then become a co-creator in form — a co-creator here on this planet, in this planetary system, in this world. And you are more, as we will always say, than you may believe to be … for there has been indoctrination that you are not of a high level but of a more lowly way and understanding. And we would say that this is not so. There may be actions taken that are not of the highest order, but this platform of experience was meant to be understood. It was meant to be understood and recognized, conceptualized, and then embraced or not by the feeling component, which you gauge throughout your meanderings on this planetary system and world.

Do recognize that there is that reckoning and that understanding, but it has been misinterpreted and reformulated, and perhaps reimagined, for there is not that full understanding but the presupposing that you are less than, that you cannot be the full measure of, and that you must relinquish your reign of control for your own body vessel to another or something that is supposed by religious doctrines that limit the expression of who you are and what you are to be.

And so we would say that, although there is no right or wrong within this planetary system in many regards, you must also be the discerner of what is what and who is who. And as you consider this, recognize that you are expansive, unbounded Spiritual Essence that has sought to take a form and to wonder no more. To now know in more certainty, or more precise mannerisms and ways, how it would be and how it would feel, to do thus and such, create thus and such, or exist simply here.

As you move about this day, look upon life as an experience. Look upon life, removing the limitations felt of what you might be able to do or not, what you might be able to experience or not, in what way and how you might exist or not, in this platform of wonderment, opportunity, and being.

Chapter 4

Purposeful Understandings and Their Undertakings

Might we begin this next chapter in a two-fold way? One, let us begin this next chapter, but also might you begin your next chapter. As you recognize that the body, the Soul, and Source Energy have come together to join this body form to facilitate what you sought to understand once before, might you recognize that there is much more within the mix of this understanding, and what will be given as we proceed?

Know that Universal Love is the key, in many regards, to all you might want to facilitate. Universal Love, as we have said, is a healing component that might be engaged in this day in a more purposeful way so that energy might be shifted in a way that you might express all you intend or intended to at one point in time.

And so how to determine the purpose you seek to find? How to determine that thing which perhaps you have only recently discovered existed? For you say, *the life purpose has been a question for quite a time, but now I have not only the life purpose but also the original purpose in which to ponder and query a question.*

And so we would say that the original purpose is the greater component and is the reason that so many have not been able to leave the Earth platform, for it is a component that must be completed for you set up the components by which the completion might occur. And so if you have not checked off all the components that would allow for that completion to exist, then you have, by the agreement that was made once, returned to consider yet again reaching that alignment and fulfilling what you set out to understand and explore once before.

We would say that once before may have been a multiple type of query or may have occurred in multiple steps in multiple times. But there is no exact formula and no exact amount of time that you need to spend on this platform except to be able to get into the flow of the awareness of what you seek to understand and sought to understand, so then its completion might be recognized.

And it is in the awareness mode of recognition that you might recognize these things would come into form and into being. For to do them and not know that you are doing them, in a manner of speaking, is by happenchance. And it is in the awareness of what you are doing, why you are doing it, and the feeling that is associated with the completion and the actual enterprise of the occurrence that is most meaningful. And so we seek now for you to recognize that this is something that has been long sought. It is because of the maya that does exist around you and the choices that do exist that seem most significant that you perhaps have not accomplished this previously.

Now we seek to share a bit more. Might you consider that in earlier times, there was an agreement? And the agreement was simply that you would do this and accomplish that. And you would recognize this by the feeling evoked in the doing of the activity.

We have spoken about the body vessel, the Spiritual Essence requiring a Soul in which to connect to this body vessel, and Source Energy that, let us say, is the glue that does then keep all components securely together. And so the Agreement is something that we would like to pause and recognize now, as it is quite significant (as) to why you are here, why you have continued to reembody, and why this life has taken the twists and turns, perhaps, that it has taken as you navigate the many varied life experiences that do exist and have existed in previous times.

The Agreement was formulated so that there was a complete understanding of what would occur and what one might expect when entering into the physicality of this domain. And so there are certain things within the

Agreement — the recognition, the understanding, the connection of the dots so to speak — so that as you move and grow and continue to navigate this life that there were certain understandings that would be accomplished.

The Spiritual Essence in the wonderment of what is, felt this was a rather easy occurrence and that it would be easily accomplished in short order. But as we have mentioned, there was not the full understanding of what this Earth experience would feel like and how the full depth of the density here would be felt, we would say, to the core.

And we have previously mentioned in other writings, and in this written way, and orally expressed that there was not the depth of understanding for the complexities of the experience and how it would be so fully felt in a most deep way. And as might be understood, it did take the Soul, in many cases, out of embodiment, for there was not the understanding that it would be in quite the way in which it was experienced and felt.

The Soul many times chose to leave the body and leave the experience. And in doing so, there was no longer the recall of that life experience. There was no longer the recall of the specific occurrences but rather the overall understanding that was gleaned in a most expedient way after the life experience had ended.

There was an overview, let us say, given, and an understanding. And as this has occurred repetitively from one incarnation to the next, and then the next, and then the other, there was a diminishment of the recall of that original objective. And although there is an understanding of the life experience and the life purpose, there is not the ready recall of the original one.

And the original one is most necessary because it is the *Original Agreement* that was made to be understood that would relinquish the rounds of reincarnation. That would relinquish and, in a manner of speaking, stop the rotation of incarnations, for the accomplishment at that point will have been completed. We would say it is the full 360-degree return of that which was initiated once upon a time, once long ago.

Once that has come to complete fruition, and the full 360-degree circle is then complete, then the Soul is no longer tethered in this way, do you see — to experience that which It sought to understand and to be understood. And so, understanding that there is an agreement, understanding that you were a participant of the Agreement, is most relevant and noteworthy.

Additionally, you were given those who would travel with you for a safe journey and would be those that you could call upon when you needed answers to questions. And the means of connection was simply that you would still the mind and connect. And initially, that was more easily attained. Yet over time, again, these beings were not seen. And so there, at this point in time, is not the recall that they do exist, although you have heard of Guardian Angels and the like. They do then travel with you to assist in answering questions. To assist to help you in many unseen ways. But you must be open to their assistance, or else how do you know you are getting that assistance or actually employing that which is beyond your mental knowingness.

We again will say that there is not a set or specific number, but we would add to say that there are usually four or five beings that are with you at all times. And of course, this number can increase because sometimes the Soul did bring Others from their dimension who did volunteer to stand behind and assist in an unseen way.

But we will say that each do have a vested interest in facilitating objectives for the Soul when the Soul is receptive to recognize that they are doing so and is looking consciously for answers that have been given that await discovery and recognition in the time and space in which they are allowed entrance. And that entrance is allowed through recognition, and conscious awareness, and employing, as we have said in other times, that ability to look and sleuth out the answers. And so will you recognize there is an agreement in place that Universe does maintain and does so Lovingly for the life experience you have asked and requested to enjoy and employ?

And so, this is the Earth platform and the means by which you understand this life occurrence. And we will say that when you cannot see these things and there is not the recall, and there is not the awareness, and there is not the early training from childhood, it is hard to know to pause the mind to elicit these things into your awareness simply because you do not know that they exist ... so how do you know you must elicit them to bring them forward?

It is a quandary, let us say, and something that is not expected, or anticipated, or brought forward in a manner that would cause you to chuckle and recognize that there are many things that are yet unknown to the mind. And so this is why we say you must step, and sidestep, and bypass the mind so that you do not limit yourself to mental ponderings or mental understandings.

We will say that because you do not recall many aspects in one time or the other that there is the inability to incorporate that which might make this Earth experience a bit easier. For if you did recall these things and knew that it was a priority, you would immediately shift your activities to do this rather than that.

But part of the journey is the discovery. Part of the journey is the mystery. Part of the journey is the unanticipated occurrences that do exist when you are here. For if you knew all these things initially, would you live your life the same way and have the same experiences that you can now claim to recall at this point in time? In other words, would you dare to dream to the extent if you knew that this was it? If you knew this was it, and you needed to enact, or do, or feel this certain thing, would you then just circumvent the other portion of the experience to get to that?

In many ways, that was the rationale of keeping this a bit cloaked, might we say. But now you have been here for a time, and more time, and there is no longer the recall. There is no longer the recall that you came to experience this or that, but really it is more that you have now become trapped within the maya that does exist within this experience and other experiences that have occurred before.

Will you recognize that although you may believe that this cause or that cause is the best thing and is something that you must get behind because perhaps you have an abundant life, and perhaps you feel that you must now give back, which we say is a good thing to do. But might you also realize that it is time to get about why you came here? For now, you have had many experiences and many opportunities, and many timelines and lifetimes of discovery. And now it is the time to move all of this forward to get about why you came here in the first place.

It is in the understanding of the three-in-one component within your body vessel, your Soul Essence, and Source — it is important to understand that they are unique and distinctly separate, one from the other. And although Soul is, in essence, Spiritual Essence and a part of Source Energy, it has taken on a form of the Soul, which makes it uniquely distinct from the other.

It is when these three come together in their formation and in the causation that does allow the experience to exist in the way, and in the manner in which it does, that you then are able to be a part of this earthbound adventure. That you are able to be a part of it in a way that blends you in to others who also are experiencing that which they perhaps are unaware, having come from a different location than the one they might suppose.

And so seek now this day to have the full understanding of what is in your future. And it is in the slowing and stilling of the mind that you can get about to find that purpose. It is in the separation of recognizing that you are not the mind — that you are not the body — that you are something more intangible than tangible — something spiritual in nature that is not equated to the physicality in which you find yourself now.

Recognize this and realize that it is for a purpose that you are here. It is for this unique purpose that you have devised, that you have come into form, and that you are experiencing the life that you have thus far experienced in this lifetime, and others, so that you might have a fuller understanding of all the different aspects that you sought to know once long ago.

We wish for you to know that there are aspects which will help you move in a manner so that you will uncover your original purpose much more quickly. And yes, we have talked about looking at childhood preferences, and those things which you sought to do before life's limitations were placed upon you. But we also seek for you to divest yourself of the mental meanderings of your mind ... for the mind does impose many of the limitations that you find in this day. And we hope first that by recognizing that the mind is a part of the body vessel, that you will understand the distinction of why the mind is not you ... for you are pure consciousness. You are consciousness and not of the physicality that the vessel and all of its components are derived.

When you recognize that you have the ability to do much more than you may currently believe ... that is the first step. For you see the recognition that you need not have the limitations that the mind has, up to this point, imposed by slowing and stopping, or stilling it for a time, then you can get about to locate that which is much more difficult without having done so. And it is much more difficult when you do not know the proper steps to take or the way in which this can be attained or achieved. And yes, you can still the mind and engage the little voice to give you the insights sought, but might there be another methodology that you might enlist and engage this day?

Might a new methodology come into play that you might engage so that you might more readily locate that which is seemingly remote, distant, or unattainable? What might that be? What might that methodology be that you could employ to activate and engage that which has been missing for a time and more time?

We expressly wish to impart an understanding which may be familiar or maybe new to you. And so, as you seek to align in this way, know there is always more that you might delve into and understand. But it is in the receptivity to receive that which is offered that often blocks the moving forward or advancement. For the mind can only calibrate or understand in a limited way.

When you seek to understand something more, we ask that you put the mind aside and perhaps adjacent to you and see it as separate from you. And that you implement any step that will allow it to move as if on a conveyor belt beyond and away from you, yet never totally detached, but let us say separate from you for a time.

And it is so there might be a greater understanding conceptualized and absorbed by this aspect of you — the personality which is in existence now. And so, will you take some deep breaths, holding to a count of three and then releasing to a count of three, so you do this for a time? And then reengage here when you are ready to proceed with this understanding.

∾ *Meditational Pause* ∾

Now that you have paused and allowed a space to be in existence … a space to be in existence from where you were before the space did occur. Might you recognize that there are understandings that you can employ to speed up the process to access that which you seek in all regards? And as you seek, so you will find.

And so, because it has been asked repetitively for this to be brought forward, it is now being brought forward into this time and space so that more might be anchored here in a way of discovery and personal truth — that these truths might perhaps set you free from the rounds of incarnation and those things that have been adopted but need not be. Need not be adopted, or implemented, or continually engaged in the rapidity of what they suggest. And let us say perhaps, what they are presumed to evoke and provoke.

For often, there is that understanding that is not real. That you must do this or that, or engage in a certain way when there is always free will, and that free will opportunity to shift-change what is placed before you. But when you do not know, or when you presume that you know all in that space, and you do not ask for more, then there is not the opportunity for more to be engaged.

Now that you have shifted, and aligned as you might, and allowed that mental pause to be engaged, and you have moved the mental knowingness aside, and out of direct correlation with what might be, we will share some unique insights that you might engage and employ and place within the day so that you align in a more specific way, and in a way that will produce all you seek, do you see?

As you have shifted the mind out of its cradle, and its position of power that arches over the body form and is that which seeks to know all, but cannot, for it is limited by the parameters by which it operates, might you move now to embrace Source Energy? That you go directly to Universe and that which is a part of the three-in-one to specifically ask in a firm but definitive way for more to be employed.

We would say as you sit in that posture, you enlist action, for this has been told before. We wish to add a caveat to it to make it even more impactful and meaningful as you navigate your day. For you see, as you engage with Source, and as you mirror the demanding yet not demanding voice and posture of enlisting that which you know to be so, enlisting that which you know is your right to know, enlisting the measure that is for your purposeful adventure to be completed and moved into its completion mode, might you sit with this query as you engage to enlist a mantra that will move this into proximity so that the mind does cease to exist, for a time, and you can then more readily connect to that which is your heart's desire? That which is your heart's means of connection. That which is more readily proffered into this three-dimensional platform. For now, you are anchoring it with a key of sorts that does unlock the energetic combination to relinquish that which is tightly held for your being and world.

This combination (when) given in sequential rhythm and Love, multiple times, and we would suggest three, it then turns — resets, turns — resets, turns and then opens the portal for you to know intrinsically, as you focus there, what it is you sought once long ago.

For you see, life is as you wish it to be. Life is that which it is, but it is so much more. It is in the wanting. It is in the energetic attachment to the desire of wanting to know and making it a pivotal point that you want this more than you want that because it is the energy of your alignment. It is the energy of your intention. It is the energy of the attention that you place upon this thing that will bring this thing into complete and full manifestation mode so that you intrinsically know … *this is it*. And then you are able to connect the dots. You are able to anchor that which was and is within your blueprint of design … for there is nothing beyond your reach. There is nothing beyond your power. There is nothing that you need not know now, for you have willed it, you have willed it into being. You have willed it to come back and resurface. You have willed it to enter into this arena of life in the here and now — today.

And so, you need not wander the desert, so to speak. You need not wander for any amount of time in the darkness and the depths of wonderment. For now is the time for you to connect, might we say, almost immediately with what you seek to proffer and know. And so, as we impart this understanding, and this mantra, will you then engage it in the wonderment and Love in which it is given? And as you add the component of trust, belief, and feeling into the mix, know that all now is possible. All now is possible as you implement the means in which you do so.

The feeling component, which is most essential, is that you know it to be so, and you accept this gift given. For it is the gift given that you then interpret what is about you, for do you see it is your gift. It is your understanding. It is your knowingness that will propel this to be brought into form. And although there may be a degree of ability to share, and direct, and guide from our vantage of limitless perspective, do you see it is your journey? It is your opportunity. It is your gift that you are to evoke and bring (this) into the physical platform in this world of form.

For to rely on another, and to rely even on Pure Consciousness and that Infinite Awareness that is unlimited and unbounded by knowledge and knowing from the vantage upon which there are insights given, that part of the journey is the discovery of the journey and the recognition that the journey is, how might we say, at the precipice of completion. And the joy of the wonderment of the understanding of what is given, and what is intrinsically received, is a part of that journey in the understanding of it.

And so, move this day. Move this day to know, and to recognize, to feel, and to embrace that which is yours to claim — that which is your energy to evoke. That which is your energy to move forward to Source Energy to say, this is mine, and I will it to know it to be; and to know and be, and have it be that which is known to be and move it now into form. Move it now into the knowingness of this form. Move it into the space where there is no longer the question but the innate, inner knowledge that *this is so*. And this resonates with the one, for it is the one that must resonate back with it. For it is an energetic commingling, do you see, of that which is and is soon to be?

And so we step back now so there is that opportunity to delve into this understanding as you move to embrace an insightful, contemplative, meditative moment to enact and ask for this which is soon to be known — which is now soon to be known — which is now … soon to be known.

Instruction —

Might you now recite this verse multiple times? Recite it as given in the manner that will elicit Universe to hear you. Know it is the recitation; it is the energy that is invoked. It is the means and methodology for this Energetic Key to become engaged.

And so, seek what avenue you might to employ that which will further anchor the ability for you to locate that which you seek to find in a manner and in the Love in which it is given.

Energetic Key

L et Light and Love remove what's amiss.
Engage that which is now time to enlist.
Move into action so that all might be,

engaged, aligned, enacted, and freed.

I seek to implore, coax, and kindly demand
to restore that which is known in-kind and in-hand.
For all which is needed in this space of time,

does embrace that mystery, both sacred and divine.

For in this day, I do seek and implore
what is inherent to my being to know evermore.
This holds a measure of what I'm soon to see —

that which is most integral, essential, vital, and key.

My purpose awaits majestic unto me
as I undertake to enlist what is soon to be.
For upon recognition when feeling my way,

I know each thing evoked will move forward without delay.

It is this connection that is essential to ascertain,
while recognizing what is soon easily attained.
I call once again to draw all in-kind,

to bubble up and resurface —

that which is intrinsically mine.

Energetic Key

I seek ...

- to engage this energetic alignment once more;
- to recognize what I might already be in the doings of, as I further explore;
- to release what awaits its cue to resurrect;
- to understand and enlist what has been lost in effect;
- to know that which I now call into full view, as I move to align with all I once knew.

Instruction —
Recite, repeat, then add to complete,
singularly, or as you feel so inclined.

Let more now be,

as I align to see

that which has awaited connection and discovery.

Let it be so,

for I am ready, awakened, and wanting to know

what it is time for me to enact, do, and be.

Chapter 5

All is Underway

As we move into this next chapter, might you contemplate on what has come before? And might you recognize that all is in the fluidity and flow and in a degree of the acceptance of your mind? For the mind does postulate and formulate and does seek to understand all ... for it perceives that it already knows all. And so as you move in this way, and recognize there is more yet to be discovered and so many things are yet to be uncovered, might you move now into this unknowingness with the mental posturing of knowing that more is yet to come?

And so, in this way, we move and progress so that you might conceptualize a bit more. And as we open now and expand the awareness from which you currently reside, might you envision that which we will describe.

Can you see Pure Consciousness, Infinite Awareness, and that which emanates from there, wanting and postulating how this or that might feel ... to be? And what does it mean to feel as one does feel in the densities which exist here? We say this is a unique and most opportune opportunity for you to experience and be in the densities of this Earth platform so that you understand how each thing you might contrive and conspire to create does feel in the creation of it. It is a unique opportunity, and one that is most special and prized in many ways — for not all can have that unique awareness in a most personal way.

And so, it was this that caused you to move into this platform of awareness and understanding. For you see, you did want to understand it in a more unique and personal way because there were those and perhaps are those components which were still unknown and wanted in a space of knowingness. And so you did enter into the Agreement from which you now reside. So you could posture and formulate pathways of purpose to enable you to see what has been gifted in this Earth journey.

And your journey has been camouflaged, might we say, so that you have the full totality of experience here. So that it is not as if you were merely visiting an amusement park where you know that the rides and the attractions are not authentic, in that you know that you are in the mix (or midst) of some activity that will return you ultimately back to where you reside. For here in this space, you feel as if this is all there is. And so, you are in a total submersion of authentic reality.

But might we say that this reality is not real? It is the unreality from which you reside. And in that lack of true form, you experience that which is not permanent and will soon be placed aside, as where you came from has no time. And so this digression, this moment in history might we say, is but a flash of light. For it does not exist as you believe it to be ... as you are here in this space.

Recognize what seems like an eternity is not that. For you came from endless and boundless, expansive enlistments of understanding. For it is here in this space where you must learn and glean that which is intrinsically important to you. And so Universe, Source Energy does say:

Well, if this one does want to know, then they will delve into the understanding and discovery of what is a more firmly footed foundational function and experience or enterprise. They will seek to know more.

And so it is from that space of wanting and sending out the intentional message to discover that which is currently a bit camouflaged and a bit inaccessible in that you must seek to want to know, rather than just merely exist in what appears in your pathway. And so might you know that all in this space is a gift of discovery? For many want to be given their answers, want to be fed and piecemealed their next step. But we tell you that the loveliness, and the bountifulness, and the expression of who you are is for you to discover. It is for you to recognize. It is for you to know when you have moved past the many opportunities and distractions that appear before you.

And when you move in that way, when you move in the way of enlisting what is most preferred and most important to you, then the keys to that understanding will be given. For you must set your vessel and your ship aright. For if you are cocked or moving in a manner that is not in alignment, that does take you off-course and on a detour, might we say, then how can you expect to suppose to land where you might propose to do so this day.

Now we move to progress another understanding that you might conceptualize or not, based on your preference to accept what is given in a Loving and reverent way. Do you see the acceptance and all that has come before is simply a choice? It is your free will choice to elicit a new understanding or to move past it and past these pages and words so that you resonate perhaps with this and not that.

Consider now that this body vessel and this Awareness have been melded and molded and are traversing this Earth, wondering, and plotting, and planning as to how to access that purpose. We will tell you that the verse given, when given in the right manner, and given from a place of conviction from the heart center, is the greatest gift we can give you now. For then, you do move into the wonderment and of the allowing of what is to be resuscitated, might we say, as it reemerges into this space and platform. For it is your insistence and the energy you evoke to bring your wonderment and understanding that you set up into being once again now.

And so, consider this. Consider this, as you in many ways see and envision this energy bubbling up from within. And then focus upon it. Focus upon it in a contemplative moment with precision, and dedication, and expectation. For if you do not believe it will come, for if you do not believe you have the ability to reenergize and move forward into the light of day those things you once wanted in a strong way, let us say, then how can it ever be reclaimed and regained by you? How can this thing ever return back to you when you do not expect it to be so?

It is in the expectation, the visualization, the meditative moments that you postulate and formulate on this one issue — this one request — this one thing, that it will bubble up and be accessible once again. For in many ways, you have chosen many paths within your lifetime that dance around the occurrence. That dance around what it is that you sought. But rather than one component, one spoke on the wheel, we would say, seek the entire wheel to roll toward you. To be expansive and energetically accessible as you tune your focus into that which is yours to claim. It is yours to know, for it is the experience that you sought to understand and feel within this earthly domain.

We seek for you to connect there. We seek for you to recognize that this is the gift given within these words and expressions that are now uniquely devised as a key so that you might unlock that which has been with you all along but perhaps not as accessible as you might prefer. For you did not know how to gain access. You did not know how to gain entry. You did not know how to bring forward that which is about you, with you, and within reach — always — all along. And so might you contemplate on this measure for a moment or two before we continue.

∾ *Meditational Pause* ∾

Now, after your pause, will you be receptive to receive? Be receptive to receive what we offer and give in Loving measure. We seek for you to have a degree of understanding and Love, and knowing that Universal Love is the bridge. It is the bridge to bring you home in many regards. And so when there is that blockage, when there is that inability to connect to receive what you perceive to be that which is rightfully yours to know — it is rightfully yours to experience and to move into that space of expression now that you have discovered its connection, might you know that Universal Love not only is the glue with which

Source Energy facilitates the anchoring of your form with your Soul Essence, now known as Soul, but it is also that energy that is the facilitator in many regards of all you seek to know? It is the means and the methodology as well as the integral energy key that will allow your verse to more synchronistically align with you.

Might you return to the verse that you received earlier and now recite these words with the component of Universal Love as its anchoring aspect. Envision it as you recite it, drawing in Universal Love to amplify, might we say, the energetic connection or key that you have been given. And now you align with it even further through the Love component … through Universal Love.

For it is not merely love as you know. It is not merely the love that is thought of as you know. It is not merely the emotional ingredient of love as you now well know. It is so much more than that … do you see? And so, now add this ingredient into the mix of that Loving combination we have given you so you might express it in the manner- ism and the way that Universe seeks for you to request what is yours to receive. For don't you see that if you ask meekly, Universe will certainly listen, but you may receive it in a rather meek way. And will you see it in its return to you? But if you do express it boldly, then Universe will pronounce it back to you in such a manner. And you are more likely to see what you need to see, must see, for this manifestation to be known by you in this time.

And so, make an assertive stance. Make an assertive stance in the energy that is most becoming of what it is you want to know. And so in that energy elicit your preference. Elicit the verse. And now do so with Universal Love as your tailwind of support as you enlist it once again now.

Instruction —

Might you recite this verse multiple times that will elicit Universe to hear you. Do so in the understanding you now hold, integrating Universal Love into this key.

Energetic Key
... *Given in Love*

L et Light and Love remove what's amiss.
Engage that which is now time to enlist.
Move into action so that all might be,
    engaged, aligned, enacted, and freed.

I seek to implore, coax, and kindly demand
    to restore that which is known in-kind and in-hand.
For all which is needed in this space of time,
    does embrace that mystery, both sacred and divine.

For in this day, I do seek and implore
    what is inherent to my being to know evermore.
This holds a measure of what I'm soon to see —
    that which is most integral, essential, vital, and key.

My purpose awaits majestic unto me
    as I undertake to enlist what is soon to be.
For upon recognition when feeling my way,
    I know each thing evoked will move forward without delay.

It is this connection that is essential to ascertain,
    while recognizing what is soon easily attained.
I call once again to draw all in-kind,
    to bubble up and resurface —
    that which is intrinsically mine.

Energetic Key
(continued)

 *I seek ...*

- to engage this energetic alignment once more;

- to recognize what I might already be in the doings of, as I further explore;

- to release what awaits its cue to resurrect;

- to understand and enlist what has been lost in effect;

- to know that which I now call into full view, as I move to align with all I once knew.

Instruction —

Now might you...

Recite, repeat, then add to complete
singularly or as you feel so inclined.
Move into cue this day without misstep or delay
in the discovery that awaits you each day.
This is our gift of Love to you.
This Love which is now indeed imbued,
as we add a degree of wonderment into the mix.

In Light & Love we do enlist
to engage what has been most remiss
as its reentry does occur in this time.
You see now all is as it might be
completing the full three sixty (360) –
as you recite, repeat, release.

Energetic Key
(*continued*)

Let more now be,
    as I align to see
    that which has awaited connection and discovery.

Let it be so,
    for I am ready, awakened, and wanting to know
    what it is time for me to enact, do, and be.

I sit now in contemplation,
    in wonderment, and expectation
    of what this purposeful understanding will reveal.

Each is as it should be,
    and thus I complete the full three sixty (360),
    as Universal Love has entered in — as the key.

Chapter 6

Completion of Your Journey Here

As we move to encircle that which has come before, know that all is as it needs to be, and as you determine what is to be, might you move with steps accordingly? So that you may bring forward all that you desire, know that your purpose purposefully awaits. It awaits your wanting. It awaits your engagement. It awaits your activation into the knowingness of what this thing, this energy is, and might evoke for you when you are consciously aware of evoking that energy. For you see, you have most probably evoked it before.

Do you see that it is in the conscious awareness of the moment, of the activity, of the engagement, of the need, and want, and desire to have known this energy that you then are moving this energy out into the world of form in a conscious sort of way? You are moving and engaging to know that which is and was unknown before at this level of knowingness. For you see, in many ways, this is the conscious awakening of the being, of the one who is nestled amongst the vessel and propagated, or propelled, or propped up by Source Energy in the alignment of the three-in-one.

Will you look upon life now in the wonderment that it is — in the wonderment that you can engage this or that activity, this or that outcome, this or that undertaking, objective, or mission? But it is when you do so consciously that the engagement becomes evolutionary. It becomes more than what it was thought to be before because now you do so not from the mere enjoyment of it but from the feeling aspect, from the true engagement of what it seeks to elicit to you in this way.

For it is your mission in many ways. It is your mission to accomplish this or that, to do so in a knowing manner, to do so with the knowingness of all that you have set out to accomplish. For you can do many things, but it is in the awareness of the doing that is so critical at this step.

For all you elicit, for all you want, for all that is to be must be done in a manner of knowing that you are doing so. It cannot be happenchance. It cannot be from the mere enjoyment of it, although we do say that life is meant to be enjoyed. But in many regards, it is the connecting of the dots … don't you see? It is connecting all the dots so that you might complete your mission and return home.

For Earth is a way station. A place where you have landed for a time, but it is not your long-term home. And if you believe in other activities, or other stories, or other past or future occurrences, you might recognize that even in Biblical understandings, you were not meant to be here always.

You were meant to be in a heavenly sort of way when you depart this life. And who is not to say that where you came from is not that heavenly way — is not that portal of potential, and possibility, and promise? For in many ways, you are not the imperfect being that you seem to experience here on this Earth platform because here the imperfections are needed to move you and shift you from this to that.

And that is why it is understood that there is no right or wrong here, for each is propelling you in a direction that is one of preference or not. It is in the proffering of the perspective and in the ability to recognize when a perspective might be shifted and may no longer be necessary — that you no longer need to look through it from a limited lens of it being this way or that. For we will say in many regards, the perspective is a part of the journey. The perspective allows you to see things from a limited vantage that are perhaps totally unfounded. But it was needed so that you might move through one and into the next. And so see life, and the perspectives kept, in this regard.

As you look upon another, know that their perspective is necessary for it is their belief. And this is why you might release beliefs. Because when you hold to a belief, and it is steadfast, you need the perspective to reinforce the belief. But when you release the belief, the perspective will yield, and shift, and move to be more in alignment with what might propel you in the next best step.

For do you see that all work in tandem — one with the other — to progress you in a way that will move you to all that your heart is desirous of. And so, if you shift this, then you will shift that. And when you release this, you will release that. And it is like a gridlock of locks. That as you go through the portal, you change the combination a bit. And in changing the combination, the gridlock is no longer in a gridlock sort of way. And now it moves to open. And you go through the next portal, and you work through that. And it opens. And you go through the next, and it opens. And all of a sudden, you see that you are before all that you seek to know. For you have allowed and shifted, and moved, and released what need not be held onto anymore at this point in time.

But all were necessary, do you see? All were necessary to move you into that space and give you the full expansive understandings you now hold. And so move this day, knowing that each thing is as it needs to be with no regret, but perhaps looking upon each thing with a new awareness … with a new understanding, with Love and an embrace from Source Energy. For you see, Source Energy is an integral component and one that is most necessary. And it is the alignment with the one that will facilitate all you seek. It is in this way that you have found the keys to release any constraints and limitations that you may find yourself imposed upon, and imposed in, and imposed with at this point in time.

And so move this day. Move this day in a purposeful way so that you might embrace the more which is to be given. The more which is always available and which you will open up to as you move beyond these pages and these words that are so given in Love.

Recognize that all of life is a play. All of life is a play that is to be enjoyed and recognized, allowing, shifting, and moving you along the path — a most purposeful path. A path that you perhaps are aligning to now know. And do not make the query difficult. Do not allow the mind to circumnavigate and say how this must be so complicated that it cannot be deciphered or understood. For we will tell you this and that, and that and this are pure folly.

They are pure folly in that the understandings are more simplistic than you may recognize or be willing to see. And it is in the simplicity and the wonderment of the simplicity that you might now embrace. Embrace that which is easily ascertained. It is not a difficult measure. But the mind seeks to relate to you that it is most difficult. And how can you ever find this thing? For it is, and has, remained hidden for a time, and more time. And so, it must be difficult if you have not been able to ascertain it before.

But we would ask, has it been your number one priority at all times for a time? And if it has not, there is no worry that it has not, but now shift and move it to be the number one objective of the day, of the week, or perhaps longer. But move it into central focus so that it is unyielding from your gaze and view. Do not limit what you think upon it. Do not limit your day so that each day you return to wondering and musing upon this thing. Recognize its unparalleled importance — its significance. And the value that this knowingness would bring to you if you were to step into the portal of understanding what it is.

We will say most likely you will have not only done it within this time, but you have done an aspect of it in another time. But perhaps not given the full reckoning of what it is and the significance along with the awareness of what you are doing and now why you are doing it. For it is the completion. It is the returning of the three sixty (360) back to you in the full awareness of what you are now engaged in and upon.

Do you see the value here? Do you see the value of recognizing that you are completing what you set out to understand? And it is in this understanding … it is in this way … it is in this undertaking that you then engage life from a more profound and resounding way.

And so, we seek your engagement now as we move into another understanding that we wish to share at this time. Recognize that all beings on Earth are not of this understanding. That there are many that have come from other systems and worlds that sought a different experience and not the life purpose, and original purpose, and the purpose-driven objectives that you find yourself amidst and in.

And these beings share the land and the space in which you share. And they do move and look just like you. They are ingrained and allowed in this space where all are allowed in per the agreement. The agreement they work out and devise. So we will say that not all here are of this understanding and persuasion. We will say that all here are not as they appear to be. And so know that as you move and engage within your day, that each walking a path has a pathway that is unique and specific to them.

If you are reading this book and in search of your purpose, most likely it is something that applies to you. But we will say to resonate upon the words that are given, and when something does not align as it might not do, then you must sit with this to allow a bubbling up of recall to surface.

For you have been taught and ingrained with a certain understanding, or perhaps you have grown into an understanding, and now something that has been said is different than that. And you wonder — *How can that be? It does not seem right? It cannot be this way or that way. It must be the way that I knew before.* But might we suggest that you release your beliefs, for many times the mind does conjecture? The mind does wage a bit of war. The mind does seek to know all and is unwilling to yield the space in which you might grow to know more.

And so we would say to sit with it. Allow it to meld and move about you and allow the consideration of the words to infiltrate your psyche and being. And then sit with it some more. And then look again. Look again and ask within the heart space that you have now anchored: *What might be so*? Ask, and find what the answer provided might be as you release the expectation for the knowingness for which you hold now.

Might you consider this in the Loving embrace we now impart? For all life here is truly the mystery and the wonderment of the engagement, of the activity for the free will component that does exist ... that does cause each to not truly know the path that will be taken at each moment of each day. There is a mystery, might we say, for you might choose this over that, and this step may move you closer, or that step may move you further away, but there is an engagement. There is an engagement of wonderment in all that does proceed as the free will component does become engaged. It does shift-change you to make this choice over that one ... to go here rather than there. And to enlist the properties and the wonderment that does exist from one moment to the next by the choices made.

Will you embrace that and recognize that these choices allow you to traverse life on a different path than perhaps yesterday would have allowed or afforded? And we do not mean that in a negative way, but we mean that each day does have new opportunities that do grow and expand from each choice made. And the beauty and the wonderment of all that is, might be, is that which it is through the choices made and proffered within each and every day.

As life does move this day, know that all is a gift. Live life in the positive framework. Recognize that each pain, each ache, each body ailment might be looked upon also as a gift as you move to embrace that which is whole and healthy as you seek to recalibrate all that is in need of a boost.

Might we play a game now where you focus on one area that is needing just that boost? And as you focus there, feel its wholeness, feel the completeness of that area. And recognize that it is purposefully and fully aligned as it might be. And that as you add a component to the mix, you add Universal Love into all that is in, around, and through that area. See Universal Love swirling amidst and about the area in question. And now envision nothing but wholeness — nothing but health and vitality — nothing but completeness in what you are viewing now in the mind's eye as you visualize its restoration and completeness as it moves in the full totality of all that it might be and more.

Will you focus upon this now for a few moments, and then we will continue?

∾ *Meditational Pause* ∾

Might we now bring forward something in a magical way into your being and world and into your existence from this point moving forward? What might you seek to know that will allow you to manifest all that your heart does desire and all that you have set into motion to move into reality, into being in the space that you now reside? What might that be? And as you have stilled the mind, have moved it away and from distraction, might you once again focus on your heart center? Might you focus there for a time?

≈ *Pause and Align* ≈

As we proceed, know that Light and Love is a gift. It is a precious gift that you can emblazon, and embolden, and express within your day when you seek to do so, do you see? And so, recognize all within life is a choice. All within life is a choice that you elect to move forward or not. That you take strides to move into the pathway of purpose and to enact but do not meander or act in a laissez-faire way that you expect it to somehow be made manifest, and you wait impatiently for that thing to become known without putting in the work to have it occur.

And do you see that when you do not make it your number one priority, it will sit in limbo, so to speak? It will sit and not advance as you might prefer it to be. And then you, in an almost insistent sort of way, wonder why it is not here … why it has not become known. Why it is not in the full expanse of what it might be otherwise.

And it is in your degree of focus, intent, and purposeful desire to bring it into manifestation. And do you see if you do not do it, who else will be the one? You cannot enlist another to do your bidding in this way. For this is your undertaking, this was your Agreement; this was your intentful desire to know this thing above *all else*. And until you rise to the occasion, then the *all else* will not be … do you see?

And so remove distraction. Remove those things that do not need to be accomplished, except mentally. Do not do those things that pacify your mind. For in the pacification of the mind, and the pacification of the allowing of the mind to let you move this way or that, seek to regain that control.

Seek to regain that which is the most important thing that you have going on right now. Recognize it supersedes most everything. And we do not mean to distract you from those obligations with family and in other internal or outer doings. But we would say that this must become the priority. This must become the allness of being and the reason that you acknowledge why you are here.

For when you move in this way, when you move in the way of knowing that you are on the precipice of such a great discovery, then you will move in an unparalleled way. You will move in an unstoppable way. You will move in a way that you perhaps have not moved before. For it is in the knowing, and the doing, and the being that this Agreement *will be no more.* You will have broken, let us say, the contractual obligation that was before you once before. And the Agreement will dissolve, for you will have reached the attainment of that which you desire.

And so move in this way this day. Move in the way of the breaking of that which is in many ways the tethering aspect that keeps you in this form, or that form, or another — until the discovery of what you set into motion has been found. And might you move with the expeditious and the all-encompassing way that this discovery will allow you to find.

And so we say, this is the offering that we give you. This is the opportunity to move forward in an unparalleled way when you connect within, still the mind, regain control, and move in that conscious way, in present moment awareness, positive thinking, and all that enacts these steps to be made manifest.

We give you our Light and Love if you will but call it into your being and world. We give you that which you desire and that which you intently and purposefully request so that you might move mountains, manifest the reality of your dreams, and bring all into fruition in this lifetime, now that you know more.

And might we say a bit more, for there is much more
that is and will be known by you in time ...

About the Elders

Think upon Us as a Consciousness of Light and Love. Think upon Us as ever-moving Light that does fluctuate and form words within the in-breath and out-breath of a beat or measure. Think upon Us as Love, in Love with all that is.

We are Love from the Consciousness of Love. We are known as those who were and are considered the Elders. This is a name that was devised a time or two ago by those who sought such knowledge according to their lineage and birth. We kept this title as it was more recently devised than others that could also have been used.

We are Beings that wish for humanity to have answers that have eluded them in recent times. There are those who have shared such information, but it is also being released in this manner, in this time, so there might be a profound knowingness as one engages with life here.

We are Pure Consciousness. We are many, and We

provide insights for humanity so that more might be gleaned in this lifetime than without such knowledge. We are Love, but all are that which is.

About the Author

Robyn G. Locke bridges the physical with the nonphysical world to bring you purpose-driven, self-healing, self-help books. She is a transformation facilitator, international speaker, energy intuitive, and spiritual seeker.

Love life. Even what appears to be bad. Discover the deeper meaning attached to each thing encountered along the way. Engage in life's mystery in this way.

These inspirational writings are given by the Elders. They provide invaluable insights and suggest refreshingly simple steps to engage. Imagine your future when mental constructs are removed and replaced with purposeful direction. Unbounded opportunities await as you consciously co-create all you desire to manifest.

About Our Books

Awaken
The Definitive Guide to Transformative Change

Awaken works in tandem with
The Greater Purpose: Awaken to Your Reason for Being

Searching for guidance that seems nowhere to be found?

Discover how to align your being and tap into those unlimited possibilities.

Do you have trouble manifesting what you want in life? Feel like you're off-course? Hurdles stopping you in your tracks? Now discover the more that awaits your future. International speaker, change facilitator, and energy intuitive Robyn G. Locke conveys wisdoms given by the Elders – Beings of Pure Consciousness and Infinite Awareness. And now she's here to share powerful Universal insights to spark the means to enact a personal renewal of ultimate self-discovery.

Awaken: The Definitive Guide to Transformative Change is the must-have handbook for seekers desiring to co-create their best life. Its many exercises, relatable stories, meditational offerings, and other insightful approaches will help you release undesired negative energy and overcome those seemingly ever-present obstacles. Utilize new understandings and their platforms of possibility and promise as you relinquish self-limiting beliefs and discover new vistas.

In *Awaken*, you'll discover:

- Ways to unlayer and remove trapped emotional energy to help you shift-change into all you might be
- Instruction on the importance of your purpose and how you can step into this new pathway with confidence and ease

- Techniques that will self-heal, create wellness, and lead you to a more lasting happiness
- How to easily, personally, and more readily transform your existence into one that manifests your dreams and desires
- The ability to access inner fulfillment, shift-change your energy, see this life differently, and so much more

Awaken is an extraordinary resource accelerating the process of true inner awareness, restorative healing, and personal transformation. If you like enacting inspirational insights, garnering a deeper understanding of Universal Love's vast capabilities and timeless teachings, then get ready for the soul-stirring results these new discoveries will bring.

Are you ready to transform into more than your mind can currently fathom?

Given in Love
How to Make This Your Last Incarnation

Ready to understand why you are here and make this the last incarnation?

Discover the pathway beyond living life here as you become consciously aware and your purpose-driven objectives become realized.

Do you desire to extend beyond your thoughts and current mental limitations? Do you understand the benefit of focusing on your heart? Want to break the endless cycle of incarnating yet again? International speaker, transformation facilitator, and energy intuitive, Robyn G. Locke holds the energetic key to connect to the Elders, vis-à-vis her Soul. Her Soul is a part of their community. These Beings seek to share in an unlimited way, so you might find your pathway beyond living life here. As a part of the Elder Community, Robyn's Soul came to remind humanity of their divinity, and why they chose to embody.

Given in Love is the means to finding your inner fulfillment, while removing self-limiting self-talk. Replace negative thoughts that cause depression, anxiety, addiction, and mental fatigue with better-feeling thoughts. Move the mind out of the way to reconnect with your deeply held divinity. When you tap into that inner truth, discover more than you might now imagine. Detach, unleash, and satisfy the Agreement as you move beyond this *Earth Experience*. Transform and restore wholeness once again.

In *Given in Love*, you'll discover —

- How to enact life with intention and the steps that will enable this to be your last incarnation.
- Ways to access a consciously aware existence that taps into the heart space.
- Your one true ambition and the purpose you sought to know.
- The means to align with that highly attuned part of you — your Spiritual Essence.

- Locate new avenues to transform, shift, and change. Discover new understandings as they surface from deep within, as your perspectives shift and new opportunities come into view.

Given in Love is a powerful guide. Its many truths are not known currently. Unearth rare wisdom and guidance chronicled within the many insights found here, and given in the Love meant to nourish both your heart and Soul. If you like profound enlightenment, straightforward advice, and resolutions enabled by the mysteries of your past, then you'll be inspired by Robyn G. Locke and the Elders' remarkable teachings. Discover now what you did not know before. For how can you truly know until you do?

**Enact steps found within *Given in Love*
to reclaim what has been lost over time!**

Connect with Us

Find us at

https://AdvancedEnergetics.org

www.Facebook.com/AdvancedEnergetics

www.Instagram.com/AdvancedEnergetics

www.YouTube.com/AdvancedEnergetics